Stop Panic Attacks in 10 Easy Steps

by the same author

How to Give Clients the Skills to Stop Panic Attacks
Don't Forget to Breathe
ISBN 978 1 84905 887 2
eISBN 978 0 85700 603 5

of related interest

Eat to Get Younger
Tackling inflammation and other ageing
processes for a longer, healthier life
Lorraine Nicolle and Christine Bailey
ISBN 978 1 84819 179 2
eISBN 978 0 85701 125 1

Recovery and Renewal
Your essential guide to overcoming dependency and withdrawal from
sleeping pills, other "benzo" tranquillisers and antidepressants
Baylissa Frederick
ISBN 978 1 84905 534 5
eISBN 978 0 85700 964 7

Breaking Free from Persistent Fatigue
Lucie Montpetit
ISBN 978 1 84819 101 3
eISBN 978 0 85701 081 0

Sleep Better with Natural Therapies
A Comprehensive Guide to Overcoming Insomnia,
Moving Sleep Cycles and Preventing Jet Lag
Peter Smith
ISBN 978 1 84819 182 2
eISBN 978 0 85701 140 4

Stop
Panic Attacks
in 10 Easy Steps

Using Functional Medicine to Calm Your
Mind and Body with Drug-Free Techniques

SANDRA SCHEINBAUM

SINGING
DRAGON
LONDON AND PHILADELPHIA

Disclaimer: Every effort has been made to ensure that the information contained in this book is correct, but it should not in any way be substituted for medical advice. Readers should always consult a qualified medical practitioner before adopting any complementary or alternative therapies. Neither the author nor the publisher takes responsibility for any consequences of any decision made as a result of the information contained in this book.

First published in 2015
by Singing Dragon
an imprint of Jessica Kingsley Publishers
73 Collier Street
London N1 9BE, UK
and
400 Market Street, Suite 400
Philadelphia, PA 19106, USA

www.singingdragon.com

Library of Congress Cataloging in Publication Data
Scheinbaum, Sandra.
Stop panicking in 10 easy steps : a practical guide / Sandra Scheinbaum.
pages cm
ISBN 978-1-84819-246-1 (alk. paper)
1. Panic disorders--Treatment. I. Title.
RC535.S34 2015
616.85'223--dc23
                    2014033804

British Library Cataloguing in Publication Data
A CIP catalogue record for this book is available from the British Library

ISBN 978 1 84819 246 1
eISBN 978 0 85701 192 3

Printed and bound in Great Britain

Contents

Acknowledgments

To the leaders in functional medicine, including Dr. Jeffrey Bland, Dr. David Jones, and Dr. Mark Hyman: thank you for your wisdom and continuing inspiration.

To my students in the Masters Program in Nutrition and Functional Medicine at the University of Western States: thank you for being my teachers as we explore the psychology of wellbeing, principles of mind-body medicine, and the psychology of eating.

To my editors at Singing Dragon: thank you for seeing the value of this book and for all your assistance and guidance.

To the hundreds of clients I've seen over the years: thank you for sharing your stories and partnering with me to overcome panic and anxiety.

Finally, thanks to Alan, Laura, Carly, and Keith for the joy, laughter, harmony, and balance you bring to my life. Keep singing, dancing, hooping, and creating beautiful music.

PREFACE
My Personal Journey from Anxious to Calm

"Calm down!"

"Get a hold of yourself."

"What's wrong with you?"

"Chill out!"

"Stop panicking!"

"Just relax!"

"Snap out of it!"

If only "snapping out of it" was simple. It isn't. But with patience combined with lots of practice, you'll stop panic and anxiety. By learning 10 simple steps, you'll experience profound changes in a short period of time. You'll stop anxious feelings from escalating into full-blown panic mode. If you've been consumed by panic and worrisome thoughts, you'll enjoy life again.

Why do I believe so strongly that you can stop panicking in 10 easy steps? Because what I'm teaching you stems from my personal experience. I used to have severe panic attacks and learned how to completely stop them. I didn't use one of the commonly prescribed anti-anxiety drugs. Nor did I engage in lengthy talk therapy. Instead, I incorporated the 10 steps outlined in this book and, by doing so, my life completely changed. I went from anxious to calm.

Anxiety started way back in early childhood. When other children went happily off to kindergarten without even glancing back at their parents, I remember crying and wanting my mother.

While my peers were learning to ride bicycles, I never even felt comfortable with training wheels. Worried that I would fall, no one could persuade me to take that leap of faith and pedal on my own. Learning to swim? Forget about it! When my mother enrolled me in a class at a local community center, I watched as, one by one, the other kids doggie-paddled away from the edge of the pool and soon became happy little guppies. Not me. Filled with terror, I didn't let go for dear life. What if I sank to the bottom? Too risky to take a chance, I remained with feet firmly planted until the class was over. Roller blade? Ice skate? No way! Held back by anxiety, I preferred less risky activities like coloring and playing with dolls.

Because my father died suddenly when I was nine, I used to worry that something would happen to my mother and I would end up in an orphanage. As a "latch-key" kid, I would stand at the window and watch for her to come home from work. If even a few minutes passed after the time she was supposed to arrive, I imagined all sorts of horrific scenarios. What if she'd had an accident? What if she was in the hospital?

In high school I worried constantly about performing well in tests and earning top grades. This is what my classmates wrote about me at graduation: "Can you imagine Sandra doing a commercial for Compoz?" (This was an over the counter anti-anxiety agent at the time.)

Why was I such a nervous wreck? Let's start with my mother: a "born worrier," just like her own mother and sister. For years I assumed that I had inherited her anxiety gene, and therefore change wasn't possible. What about stressful life events? Couldn't my anxiety be attributed to losing my father at an early age? Certainly that trauma didn't help, but I exhibited signs of anxiety years before his death. So what else was going on? Maybe it wasn't all due to bad genes or childhood trauma. Maybe there were other factors at play. When the body becomes out of balance, how can the mind stay calm? From infancy on, all signs pointed to significant imbalances. Bottle-fed and colicky as a baby, I also suffered from frequent ear infections, tonsillitis, and bladder infections as a young child, necessitating course after course of antibiotics. My favorite meals consisted of bologna slices on white bread or buttered noodles, plus frequent treats of cookies, candy, and ice cream.

As we'll discover in the later steps, a healthy, happy gut is key to a healthy, happy mental state. Because I was bottle-fed, my microbiome, the diverse colony of bacteria that live in the gut, may not have been adequately populated from day one. Adding insult to injury, the beneficial bacteria I did possess were decimated by the triple whammy of antibiotics, a sugar-laden, highly processed diet, and the psychological trauma of losing my father. Worrying created further gut imbalances, setting me up for more anxiety.

My frequent consumption of sugar morphed into a full-blown addiction in college. After stuffing myself with candy from the school vending machines, cookies left out by the kindly house matron in my sorority house, unlimited desserts served at meals, and late night pizza and pasta orders, I felt disgusted with myself and often attempted to eat what I considered to be healthy food the following day: carrots and fruit (foods which, alas, also turn to sugar).

These dysfunctional eating patterns fueled my anxiety, but I didn't know that back then. As I filled up on sugar, quality proteins, good fats and vegetables were crowded out (how could I choose a food like broccoli when brownies were calling my name?). As a result, I lacked the necessary building blocks for brain health. To make matters even worse, I engaged in no form of physical exercise. A serious student, besides walking to and from classes, I spent my days studying. Yoga and relaxation techniques weren't widely available, and certainly not offered on a college campus in the 1960s. As if being nutritionally depleted and lacking exercise weren't bad enough, I started on yet another long course of antibiotics to clear up an outbreak of acne. So what kind of shape do you think my gut was in by this time?

Binging on sugar continued unabated while working on my master's degree. What better way to relieve the stress of test taking and paper writing than with some ice cream? Plus who knew that my "healthy" breakfast cereal or pasta for dinner was turning into sugar as well? After graduate school, newly married and teaching a class of children with severe behavioral disorders, I continued to make bad food choices and never exercised. How convenient that I always had a supply of cookies in the classroom cupboard for snack time. Stopping at an ice cream shop on my way home from a long day at work became a regular habit.

The onset of full-blown, debilitating panic attacks began in my mid-twenties. These episodes were so bad that I often had to go to the emergency room because I thought I was dying. One experience particularly stands out in my memory.

My husband and I were spending the first winter in our new house in a Chicago suburb. There was a huge blizzard one evening and in the morning snow continued to fall. My husband left for work very early, although the driveway was already almost impassable. Because the schools were closed I had no work and was happy to be at home. The snow kept falling all morning and into the afternoon. Worried about being snowed in, I decided to shovel the driveway. Now this was an activity that I didn't engage in on a regular basis. In fact, having grown up in an apartment building, I had only shoveled snow once before. Although the snow was quite deep, I made slow but steady progress down our long driveway. About midway, I decided to go into the house to warm up. I remember thinking about the warnings regarding the dangers of shoveling snow. That's when the panic attack happened.

I started having difficulty catching my breath and immediately noticed a feeling of light-headedness. I felt scared and noticed that now it was even harder to breathe. I thought again about how people have heart attacks due to shoveling snow. Lo and behold, I noticed that my left arm seemed numb. This observation frightened me because I thought my heart was vulnerable, a conclusion I erroneously came to since learning I had a heart murmur at around age five. Now I felt chest pain and it occurred to me that I was alone in the house in the middle of a blizzard and having a heart attack. It seemed like I was going to pass out. I thought about dying from a heart attack even though I was only 25 years old. The shortness of breath and chest pains escalated, so I called 911.

By the time the ambulance arrived, my heart rate was sky high and I still couldn't catch my breath. The paramedics took over and soon I arrived in the emergency room by stretcher. After an EKG, the emergency room physician informed me that I hadn't suffered a heart attack. Instead, the nurse handed me a paper bag and instructed me to breathe into it. Finally convinced that I was OK, I let go of the panicky sensations. By that time, my frantic husband had arrived. Feeling embarrassed and silly, I joked with him about the incident, and the anxiety eased even more.

I had worked myself up into a classic panic attack. There were other episodes as well. Walking down a busy street on a vacation, I suddenly felt dizzy and had difficulty breathing. Sitting in a theater watching a play, I noticed chest pains and worried about having to leave and disrupt the audience. After taking my first aerobics class, I debated with myself whether or not to proceed straight to the emergency room because I again believed I was having a heart attack.

When I saw my physician and told him about my heart palpitations and difficulty breathing, he found nothing physically wrong, but prescribed a drug called Inderol. After filling the prescription, I did some investigating and learned that Inderol is a beta-blocker and commonly prescribed for hypertension, chest pain, irregular heartbeat, and migraine headaches. Wow! Taking this medication would reinforce one of my worst fears: that I had inherited a heart condition. This route was not for me, so I threw the pills away. I remember thinking that there must be a better way to calm down. Thus began my journey towards healing.

Coincidentally, around that time I began a doctoral program in clinical psychology and enrolled in a workshop about mind-body medicine. The course incorporated the concept of breathing for relaxation and students were led through a variety of relaxation experiences in class. As a chest breather, like most people with panic, I initially struggled to find a quieting response. But I knew that the mind-body strategies I was learning were powerful and could yield game changing results. By incorporating these techniques I could control panic and anxiety, so I kept practicing and soon had a vast repertoire of physical and mental relaxation strategies to call upon. That was over 30 years ago. I haven't had a panic attack since.

Over the years, I continued to study mind-body medicine and gathered a variety of methods for achieving inner peace. Some of these came from cognitive-behavioral therapy, others from mindfulness training and positive psychology. I discovered the important connection between food and anxiety and between exercise and anxiety, so I radically changed my diet and began to work out regularly. I fell in love with yoga and trained to become a yoga instructor. With each new step, I found even more wellbeing.

Then one day, I stumbled upon the website of the Institute for Functional Medicine and decided to attend one of their conferences. Here was a transformational way of thinking about chronic illness that looks at root causes, rather than just naming the condition and prescribing a particular treatment. What's the difference between this approach and the conventional route?

The conventional physician I saw all those years ago listened to my description of symptoms, labeled my condition as panic disorder, and prescribed medication. This process isolates anxiety from what's going on in the rest of the body, as well as "under the hood" at a metabolic level. As a psychologist, albeit one who advocated mind-body therapies, I was guilty of the same sort of reductionist thinking. Substituting relaxation techniques for medication to treat panic, while ignoring other physiological symptoms or underlying dysfunctions, wasn't getting at the root causes that drive anxiety. Functional medicine addresses these underlying factors. That's why my accidental discovery of functional medicine was such a life-changing experience.

Suppose I had seen a functional medicine practitioner after my first panic attack. He or she would have created a timeline that chronicled my story, noting that I had a family history of anxiety, was bottle-fed, took a lot of antibiotics, was traumatized by the death of a parent, developed a sugar addiction, lacked exercise, was likely vitamin D, protein, and omega 3 fat deficient, and had a high amount of work and school-related stress. Next my poor digestive health, underactive thyroid, high blood glucose levels, and panic attacks would have been viewed as a matrix of interconnected dysfunctions rather than isolated conditions. Toxic load would have been considered, as I had a mouthful of mercury dental fillings and possible exposures to other heavy metals and contaminants.

When explaining my story back to me, a functional medicine practitioner would have discussed the likelihood that a diet high in sugar, gluten, dairy, and diet sodas was fueling inflammation and creating disturbances in important metabolic pathways so that my brain was now "on fire." A plan for healing my digestive tract, cooling the flames of underlying inflammation, even helping my cells produce energy more efficiently would have been initiated. The value of incorporating mind body strategies, not just to stop a panic attack, but also to create physiological changes on a cellular level, would have been emphasized. With this functional medicine approach, the root causes, rather than just the symptoms of panic, would have been treated.

After that first workshop, I enrolled in every course offered through the Institute for Functional Medicine and am proud to be a member of the first graduating class (and the first clinical psychologist) of Certified Functional Medicine Practitioners. Not only did discovering functional medicine change my life, it also transformed the way I work with clients.

The 10 steps presented in this book are based on a functional medicine way of thinking combined with basic principles of mind-body medicine, cognitive-behavioral therapy, and positive psychology. The techniques that you'll learn have helped the hundreds of clients who came to me during the 35 years that I've been practicing as a clinical psychologist. I have successfully taught these strategies to young children as well as older adults who suffered from panic for many years.

I want this book to serve as a practical, how-to guide that you can turn to for the strategies that work best for eliminating panic and anxiety. In the following steps I'll teach you how to stop a panic attack and let go of worrying: my old demon. These methods work. And what's more, they're surprisingly simple. That's why you can learn them in just 10 easy steps. But it's not meant to be "one size fits all." Some personal favorites will emerge. Practice and incorporate all of them, or just focus on your "top picks" to relax your body and quiet your mind.

STEP 1
Let Go of "Fearing Fear"

RECOGNIZE THE BODILY SENSATIONS ASSOCIATED WITH PANIC

Do any of these experiences sound familiar?

- "My heart is racing so badly that I think it'll explode."

- "I feel like I'm going to faint at any minute."

- "I have difficulty catching my breath and can't speak."

- "There's numbness and tingling up my arms and legs like pin pricks."

- "My chest aches."

- "My mouth is so dry I'm unable to talk."

- "My hands feel wet and clammy."

- "I feel as if I'm choking to death."

- "I get cramps and muscle aches."

- "It feels like I'm in a state of constant tension."

- "I feel jittery and can't settle myself."

- "It feels like I stayed up all night even though I got enough rest."

- "It seems like I'm having a 'caffeine high' even though I didn't drink any coffee."

- "It feels as if everything is unreal, like I'm having an out-of-body experience."

- "I notice ringing in my ears."

- "I feel dizzy and light-headed."

- "My arms and legs are shaking and I can't make them stop."

- "I feel like I can't walk."

- "It's like my legs are buckling underneath me."

If you experience any of these symptoms and have never had them evaluated by a physician, the prudent course of action is to first get a thorough check-up to rule out a serious medical condition. When your doctor tells you there's nothing physically wrong, then begin Step 1. Start by saying to yourself, "It's just panic."

The feelings described above reflect just some of the ways our bodies respond during a panic attack. While they're happening, these sensations are definitely very scary, but the good news is that they're just signs of panic and you can get rid of them. We're going to discuss in great detail how to deal with these sensations when they appear. Better yet, once you learn to stop a panic attack and significantly reduce anxiety, these symptoms will vanish. Although it may seem hard to believe, you can accomplish this without medication or a prolonged period of time in therapy.

RECOGNIZE THE PROGRESSION TO "FEARING FEAR"

The following statements are frequently voiced by those anxiety-sufferers who progressed to Level II Panic. Do any of these fears sound familiar?

STEP 1

- "I'm afraid that these feelings will come over me, as if out of nowhere."

- "I worry about not being able to function because I feel so bad all the time."

- "I'm embarrassed and ashamed because of how I feel."

- "I think I'm the only one who has these crazy, scary sensations."

- "I feel like I'm going crazy."

- "I think I'm having a nervous breakdown."

- "I'm afraid I might have to go see a psychiatrist."

- "I'm afraid I'll have to take medication."

- "I'm afraid I might be put in a psychiatric hospital."

If you're saying these words to yourself, or describing these types of thoughts to others, then you've progressed to Level II: making yourself anxious about being anxious. The longer the symptoms associated with panic are experienced, the more likely it is that worrying about having anxiety preoccupies your thoughts. Having a panic attack becomes one of your biggest fears.

Why is recognizing and accurately labeling "what is" so important? By doing so, you've positioned yourself to prevent progression to "fearing fear." When you're anxious about being anxious, maybe you think twice about engaging in an activity or going to a particular place where you previously had a panic attack. I refer to these states as "overlays," or fear of fear. In other words, panicking about the possibility of having a panic attack. Once you start engaging in avoidance behaviors or worrying about when a panic attack might occur, these "overlays" often become worse than the original panic episodes that preceded them.

STEP 1

For example, you may:

- avoid driving

- turn down social invitations

- stop going to the grocery store

- avoid sitting in the center of a row at the movies

- take a seat near the exit

- avoid crowds

- stay away from restaurants

- avoid public speaking

- prefer staying at home

- fear exercising.

From now on, label these avoidance behaviors as nothing more serious than bad habits, just like a tendency to slouch or clench your jaw. After a bad experience, it's perfectly natural to want to avoid repeating it. Soon this pattern becomes habitual. But, if you've developed a bad habit, you can learn and then practice new ways of thinking and acting, and, as a result, the old habits become less pronounced. By practicing new learning over and over again, better habits replace older, more dysfunctional ones that weren't serving you well.

BUT I'M ON MEDICATION

- "I'm afraid to not take my meds."

- "I tried to get off and felt too anxious."

LET GO OF "FEARING FEAR"   19

- "I've been on this medication for many years and my doctor wants me to stay on it to prevent anxiety."

- "I'm afraid I'll get a panic attack when I'm go out, so I take the medication just to be on the safe side."

- "I hate taking drugs, but I heard it was too hard to get off."

- "I've been told I'll need to be on medication for the rest of my life."

What's the medication really doing for you? Here's what I tell my clients:

Imagine young children who don't yet know how to swim. In order to be safe while in the water, they wear a flotation device around their upper arms commonly referred to as "water wings." Water wings enable a non-swimmer to get in the water and stay safe. What happens when children learn to swim? They typically take off like guppies and no longer need water wings. But some children like the security of the water wings, so the air can be let out gradually until they feel confident enough to swim on their own.

Anti-anxiety medications act like water wings. Do you want to be wearing water wings for the rest of your life or do you want to learn how to swim? Learning how to quiet your mind and body is like learning how to swim.

Medications lose their effectiveness the longer you take them. Sometimes you may need higher doses to get the same effect. That's like needing bigger and bigger water wings. Sometimes your physician recommends adding a second drug. So now you're encumbered with wearing an inner tube in addition to the water wings. Medications often have side effects. That's like getting a skin irritation from the water wings. Medications may not always work. That's like having to deal with a broken or leaky flotation device. Maybe now you've developed anxiety about the possibility of your water wings malfunctioning.

STEP 1

Consider the process of learning how to swim. It's scary at first to come away from the edge of the pool and lift your feet off the bottom (a childhood experience I remember all too well). But once you're floating or doggie-paddling, the rest just involves refining your technique and learning new strokes. With practice, swimming becomes automatic. You're able to get in the pool and glide through the water without thinking about the mechanics of each stroke. Each time you get in the pool, you don't think to yourself, "Will I know how to swim today?" or "What if I can't swim today and need water wings?"

Similarly, when you initiate these 10 easy steps for stopping panic and anxiety, it'll be challenging at first and you may worry that they won't be effective. But if you don't give up, and faithfully continue to practice the steps, new neural pathways form in your brain so that stopping a panic attack becomes automatic. In fact, you won't feel panicky because you'll be used to a new way of being. You won't "get in the pool and forget how to swim." Your body will know how to maintain a quiet state because of all that practice. You'll feel confident because you "know how to swim."

TELL YOURSELF YOU'RE CREATING PERMANENT CHANGE

Why bother working so hard to relax when quick relief comes from swallowing a pill? The answer to that question can be found by turning to the science of hope: the study of neuroplasticity, cell turnover, and gene expression.

Neurologist Dr. David Perlmutter, author of *Grain Brain* (2013) talks about neural networks as plastic, dynamic architecture. Picture them as constellations of neurons that light up momentarily to perform a specific task. When generating a specific thought, correlating neural networks are reinforced. When you repeatedly engage in the same bad habits, neural pathways are reinforced over

STEP 1

and over again. If anxiety becomes a way of life, the brain grows accustomed to these states. With each new fear-producing episode that specific neural network strengthens, so the toxic thoughts and emotions, as well as the panic reaction associated with that network, become more entrenched.

Rewire Your Brain

Neuroscience research demonstrates that you can grow new brain cells and actually change the neural networks. The human brain has the ability to rewire itself and form new connections between neurons. Neuroplasticity, the term used to describe the brain's ability to create new neural networks, means that the brain is capable of change and continues to change throughout life.

It's possible to alter brain function so as to permanently let go of panic. By not activating the circuitry currently associated with the panic response, the brain will stop using those networks. Rather than reinforcing the anxiety pathways, you can build the neural pathways for joy and inner quiet and express the genes associated with health and wellbeing. How does this happen? Rewiring the brain's circuitry and creating positive neural pathways involves following my 10 Easy Steps program.

New neural networks are strengthened by focused, sustained attention. It's not enough just to dabble in active stimulation; building new pathways requires continual practice. Think of how you master any skill, such as learning to play the piano. No one becomes an accomplished pianist by sitting down at the piano a couple of times. No one learns a piece of music by getting partway through and then walking away. Yet that's how many people approach mastering panic and anxiety. They may practice a calming technique on a few occasions and conclude that "it's not working," or begin to practice, notice an uncomfortable sensation, give up, and go for the pill.

In addition to creating new neural pathways, your brain can grow new neurons, a process known as neurogenesis. Due to cell turnover,

STEP 1

dying cells are replaced with new neurons. The brain constantly replenishes itself with new stem cells that can be converted into fully functional brain cells. Brain-derived neurotrophic factor (BDNF) plays a key role in neurogenesis. Here's the good news: you have control over the factors that influence DNA to produce this protein. They include full mental engagement, or mindfulness, exercise, and "brain foods" such as fish oil (all part of the 10-step program). How exciting that we can stimulate neurogenesis and strengthen the neural pathways that bring about positive changes!

Bringing about permanent changes requires patience in addition to diligent practice. Some effects of following the 10 steps will be observed immediately, but others may not appear until six months to a year from now or even longer. If you accept the concept of change as a lifelong process, then begin viewing yourself as on a continual path of transformation.

You can even transform your genes. While the genetic code doesn't change, genetic expression does. Genes receive signals to turn on or off. Anxiety may "run in the family," but whether it's expressed depends on current lifestyle factors. Although my mother, grandmother, and maternal aunt were all chronic worriers, none of them knew how to take slow belly breaths or change their catastrophic thinking. They didn't practice yoga or meditate, and they didn't use food as medicine. Just because anxiety may "run in the family," it's not your destiny. Other disorders aren't your "lot in life" as well. To learn more about how you can influence your genetic makeup, I recommend reading *The Disease Delusion* by Dr. Jeffrey Bland (2014).

Neuroplasticity, neurogenesis, and gene expression all suggest that the brain can change in positive ways. So if you need to stay on medication, use it as short-term "water wings" while you practice taking the 10 steps towards swimming on your own. Use these powerful new "medicines" to move with ease through any rough waters ahead.

STEP 1

STEP 2
Recognize Panic as Your Alarm System at Work

YOU'RE NOT PHYSICALLY OR MENTALLY ILL

Do these statements sound familiar?

- "I went from doctor to doctor trying to find out what was wrong with me."

- "I'm not convinced that this isn't physical."

- "These symptoms are too severe to be just from anxiety."

- "My doctor referred me to one specialist after another and they put me through a lot of expensive tests, but nothing was positive."

- "I start feeling sick when I'm feeling relaxed, so there must be something going on besides anxiety."

- "I don't trust that these attacks are just anxiety, so I made an appointment with my doctor to get everything checked out just in case something shows up."

- "I asked my doctor for more tests because I'm hoping that he'll find what's wrong to explain why I'm feeling like this."

- "If it's not physical, then I must be going crazy."

How many doctors have you been referred to, sought out on your own, or considered seeing due to your symptoms? If you suffer from panic, it's not atypical to have seen all of the following specialists:

- cardiologists

- gastroenterologists

- endocrinologists

- neurologists

- pulmonary specialists

- rheumatologists

- psychiatrists.

Because the symptoms associated with panic are physical, it's hard to be convinced that a physical illness isn't present. I've often heard panic-sufferers say that they wished for a medical diagnosis. That knowledge would bring peace of mind and a possible route to effective treatment.

Do you accept that your symptoms don't reflect a physical disorder, but believe you have a mental illness? The medical community focuses on finding a name for what's wrong with you. If your list of complaints matches "panic disorder" or "generalized anxiety disorder," then one or both of those labels get assigned to you. Since these conditions fall under the larger category of "mental and psychiatric disorders," now you have a mental illness.

Based upon listening to hundreds of clients describe the needless suffering they've brought upon themselves after receiving a "psychiatric illness" diagnosis, I came to the conclusion that these labels do more harm than good. When you believe that you're mentally ill, what happens to your capacity to imagine feeling better? How much more likely are you to accept that you'll be "sick" the rest of your life and need medication to manage the symptoms? How

STEP 2

about the possibility that this diagnosis leads to more fears and anxieties? Maybe you're worried that you may not be able to work or lead a normal life. You may feel embarrassment or shame, and fear that others will find out that you're mentally ill. Maybe you fear that your children will inherit your "disease."

From now on, repeat this sentence: "I'm not mentally or physically ill." Panic attacks have nothing to do with malfunction. In fact, the exact opposite occurs. Every system in your body is working perfectly to protect you.

UNDERSTAND HOW YOUR ALARM SYSTEM WORKS

In the late 1970s, I attended a lecture given by Dr. Judith Greene of the Menninger Foundation during which she explained the workings of the sympathetic branch of the autonomic nervous system. I loved the simplicity of her dramatic example and so have my clients, as it brings instant understanding of what panic actually means, thereby initiating a healing journey.

So follow this imaginary tale to understand the panic response:

- Pretend that it's late at night and you're on your way home.

- As you turn onto your street, you notice that the streetlights are off and it's pitch black.

- You walk towards the entranceway in complete darkness.

- Suddenly you feel something around your ankle. *It's a snake!*

Imagine how you feel at that moment. Gripped by fear, your heart pounds in your chest and you can't catch your breath. Maybe you feel tightening in your stomach or notice that your arms and legs are numb.

STEP 2

You just activated the "fight or flight" mechanism, our biological response to danger. This system works beautifully to protect us. Imagine it's thousands of years ago and you're walking through the forest. Suddenly you notice a saber-toothed tiger headed straight towards you. At that moment, you have only two choices: either stay where you are and fight for your life or turn around and run for your life as fast as you can. That's why it's called "fight or flight."

The cardiovascular system works hard during the fight or flight response. In order to efficiently fight or run away from imminent danger, you need blood supply to the appropriate muscle groups and internal organs. Therefore, your heart beats faster to accomplish this. Blood is directed away from the places in your body that aren't directly involved in fighting or running so it can be used for the emergency. For example, it's shunted away from your hands and feet, the surface of your skin, and the parts of your brain that have to do with planning, reasoning, and concentration. The latter occurs because fighting or running away are reflex actions that don't require thinking or planning.

How else does the body protect you during this emergency? You take quick gasps of breath through your upper chest because that's the fastest way to get oxygen. Your vision and hearing may become particularly acute to sense danger. Your muscles contract to fight or run away. Increased sweat gland activity may occur because the body knows that you're working hard while fighting or running away and its important to stay cool.

What systems are put on hold? It's not important to digest your food when that animal is running after you, as all your energy must go towards fighting or running away. Therefore, digestion gets put on hold. This happens even at the level of saliva production; hence a dry mouth may occur during the emergency. Similarly, the important work conducted by your immune system isn't crucial when you're facing imminent danger. So fighting toxins, viruses, and other microscopic invaders gets postponed until the immediate and greater threat passes.

STEP 2

Every part of your body engages in the fight or flight response. Some are directly involved with the battle, while others are in a holding pattern so that all resources can be directed to the emergency.

Now let's go back to the snake that's coiled around your leg:

- Imagine that a light comes on.

- You look down, and, instead of a snake, see a coiled garden hose.

Notice how different you feel now that you're out of danger. On a biological level, your body gets the message that the tiger has moved off in another direction. Gradually you can breathe again and your heart begins to slow down. Slowly, all systems return to normal. The body goes back to digesting food, the immune system resumes its work, and blood flows back to your hands and feet as well as the brain centers responsible for problem solving.

But if it was just a garden hose all along, and not a snake, what triggered the fight or flight response?

The word "snake."

What was responsible for stopping the fight or flight response?

The words "garden hose."

Very simply, think of every word you say to yourself, every thought, and every mental image as a shower of chemicals generated in your brain. Imagine that they're processed through a massive sorting system, sort of like two laundry bins: one for darks and one for lights. There's no in-between. Every word and image must go into one or the other. Where did the word "snake" go? Because you associate snakes with danger, it went into the dark pile.

The hypothalamus-pituitary-adrenal axis picks up the danger signal. Adrenaline, a hormone secreted by the adrenal glands, activates the sympathetic branch of the autonomic nervous system. Think of adrenaline as the first responder at the scene of an accident.

STEP 2

At this point, the cardiovascular system starts to work harder to pump blood to the muscle groups involved in fighting or running away, and the entire cascade of responses described earlier is set into motion. Remember, these actions represent the body just doing its job: responding intelligently to protect you from a perceived threat.

Imagine walking around with a built-in alarm system, a home alarm device that's armed and ready to activate 24 hours a day. When a particular thought or mental image is sorted into the danger pile, you've put your finger on the home alarm switch to signal that there's an emergency, so the siren blares.

THE ALARM SYSTEM WORKS AS QUICKLY AS A REFLEX

An emergency response team must work quickly. The tiger is coming towards you and there's no time to lose. Therefore, the fight or flight response must operate as quickly as a reflex, as fast as the reaction that takes place when you accidentally touch a hot stove. It's easy to forget this important point in the midst of a scary panic attack.

What if you believe that your panic attacks "come out of nowhere"? Have you ever found yourself just walking down the street or standing in line at the supermarket and the panic just hits you? This assumption that panic "hits you from the blue" stems from the lightning quick speed of a reflex. But by dissecting the process to find the panic-producing thought or mental image, the cycle becomes clear.

The word "snake" or mental picture of a snake equals pressing the emergency switch on an alarm system. The alarm system doesn't know that it's a false alarm, so it directs the body's survival mechanism to gear up for fighting or running away. Everything happens in a split second, so it's often hard to see the connection between your thoughts and the body's intense physical responses to them. Likewise, once in the throes of a panic attack, you may not

STEP 2

be aware that you're continuing to generate a stream of negative thoughts. Here's a common scenario that exemplifies this process:

- You feel panicky so you start taking deep breaths.

- But you notice that you're still feeling your heart pounding or your knees about to buckle under you, so you tell yourself that breathing isn't working.

- Then you attempt to distract yourself by turning on the TV or listening to music but you can't concentrate because the panicky feelings are too strong.

- Therefore, you conclude that breathing doesn't work and neither does distraction.

What's wrong with this picture? In the throes of panic, you didn't realize, or forgot to take into account that the panic response, because it's actually the fight or flight survival response, develops instantaneously. But the relaxation response takes time to develop. When you initiate any strategies to stop the panic, such as breathing or distracting yourself, the symptoms will continue for a period of time. That's because the fight or flight response can only be replaced by the calming response in a very slow fashion. One negative thought, such as "breathing isn't working," or "I'm still feeling anxious," gets interpreted as a "danger" signal, so the cycle continues and you still feel panicky.

WAIT PATIENTLY WHILE THE ALARM SYSTEM TURNS OFF

Compare a panic attack to a home alarm system being accidentally triggered. With lightning quick speed, emergency vehicles arrive at the scene. Suppose you say to the police and firefighters, "Never mind; it's a false alarm." Do you think they're going to quickly turn

STEP 2

around and leave without thoroughly checking the building from top to bottom? They'll stick around for a long time to make sure everything's safe, and so will your stress hormones. Once activated, adrenaline takes its time clearing from your body.

If you walk into a room and flip on a master light switch, the room is instantly lit. That's the panic response. The relaxation response resembles going from room to room shutting down each individual lamp separately.

The key to stopping panic attacks involves turning snakes into garden hoses so you don't trigger the alarm system. If it's accidentally activated, realize you've created a false alarm and wait patiently until the emergency responders leave.

In the following steps, I'll teach you how to change snakes to garden hoses and keep the brake on the alarm system by changing your thoughts and images, and simultaneously relaxing and nourishing your body.

STEP 2

STEP 3
Take Slow Belly Breaths

If I had to choose the quickest and most effective way to stop a panic attack, taking some slow belly breaths would win hands down. But, when in the throes of a panic attack, remembering to breathe may be the last thing you're focusing on.

IS YOUR BREATHING PATTERN DYSFUNCTIONAL?

Four dysfunctional breathing patterns are commonly associated with anxiety.

1. Shallow Chest Breathing

What's the normal breathing pattern during a panic attack? Your body needs oxygen as fast as possible to allow you to fight hard or run away fast. So you rapidly draw in air by lifting your upper chest. You may feel your shoulders lift if you take a chest breath. When exaggerated, it looks like gasping for air. Nearly 100 percent of people who suffer from anxiety breathe with their chest.

Lifting your chest to take a deep breath may feel comfortable, but it's not the natural way to breathe. Did you ever watch infants or small children breathe? Their tiny bellies move in and out. They only take chest breaths while crying or upset. With practice, you can use your belly to initiate each breath, just as you were doing when you were an infant.

2. Inhaling More than Exhaling

A second, but related, pattern of dysfunctional breathing consists of excessively focusing on inhaling, especially if you're short of breath or light-headed. Feeling as if you can't get enough air, you may think you need to inhale strongly, usually by lifting your chest. Then, because you're focused on the need for more air and often worried that you can't breathe, you inhale again to get more air.

What happens when you keep repeating this type of breath cycle? You hyperventilate! Hyperventilation occurs when you inhale and don't take the time to exhale fully. Inhaling again before the lungs empty of carbon dioxide causes the build-up of too much oxygen. That's why the fastest way to stop an extreme panic attack consists of breathing into a paper bag.

Find a steady rhythm of breathing by keeping the exhalations as long as the inhalations to prevent hyperventilation. The exhalation is the most relaxing part of the breath, so prolong and savor it to fully experience the process of "letting go."

3. Holding Your Breath

A third breathing pattern contributing to panic involves holding your breath. Directly connected to fear, you may suddenly gasp and then freeze, like a deer caught in headlights. Forgetting to breathe is also associated with complete absorption in worrisome thoughts.

4. Breathing Too Rapidly

The fight or flight response needs rapid breathing. If a wild animal is chasing you, your body requires a lot of oxygen very quickly to fight or run away. This may look like shallow, panting breaths.

STEP 3

FROM PANICKY TO RELAXED BREATHING
Breathe with Your Belly

When you take slow belly breaths your body gets the message that you're not in danger, so you'll turn off the alarm system. First make sure you're breathing with your belly.

- To begin the process of breathing for relaxation, start by placing one hand on your stomach and the other hand on your chest.

- Take a big breath in and notice if you lifted the hand resting on your chest more than the hand resting on your stomach.

- Now take the next breath by pushing out your belly so that you can feel the hand on your stomach rise.

- Then draw your belly towards your spine and observe your stomach sinking down.

Just observe your stomach moving out and in. If you're thinking that you can't breathe with your stomach and need to lift your chest to get air, these negative interpretations will stand in your way because they're triggering a stress response. As a result, your body will want to take a chest breath. Instead, tell yourself that learning to breathe abdominally takes practice and you're a beginner student.

Technically, abdominal breathing means diaphragmatic breathing. When you push out your belly, the diaphragm, which is a sheet of muscle below your ribcage, pulls down. This process allows air to be "sucked in" to your lower lungs. When you lift your chest to get air, the diaphragm isn't engaged and air only fills your upper lungs. Belly breathing results in getting air into both your upper and lower lungs. That's why singers and musicians who play wind instruments are taught abdominal breathing.

When I teach belly breathing, I often hear comments such as "I'm not getting enough air this way." In reality, engaging your abdomen to draw in breath gives you more air. Try inflating a balloon

STEP 3

by just inhaling through your chest. You'll get less air into the balloon than if you engaged your stomach by pushing it out and then slowly drawing it back in order to release air into the balloon.

Inflating and deflating a balloon serves as a great image for mastering abdominal breathing.

- Imagine your stomach is a balloon that you're going to blow up with air as you inhale.

- Imagine your stomach is a deflating balloon as you exhale. See if you can lose yourself in this image for several more breath cycles.

- Observe your shoulders. Are they rising and falling with each inhalation and exhalation? If so, tell them to stay still.

- Observe your thoughts. Is your mind judging, evaluating, or complaining at this moment? If so, remember that all thoughts and mental images are sorted into darks and lights, safety or danger.

- Replace negative thoughts with positive, encouraging ones.

- Tell your mind that it's the observer. Imagine you're doing an experiment and your mind is functioning like a scientist. You're simply observing the process of breathing.

- If your mind wanders, bring it back to noticing the very next breath.

- If you observe that you're breathing with your chest, simply observe that process and take advantage of the next breath to try an abdominal pattern.

Here's another visualization that may be helpful when learning belly breathing.

STEP 3

- Imagine that there's a string attached to your navel and it's being gently pulled away from the body. Feel that as the inhalation.

- To exhale, imagine there's a string attached to your navel from the inside and you're gently pulling the string towards your spine.

Practice belly breathing as often as possible. Start with times when you're comfortable or happy and experience those good feelings deepening as the breath deepens. Whenever you're feeling contentment, and wish to savor the moment, take a deep abdominal breath. For example, when you walk outside and it's a beautiful day, enhance the positive experience with belly breathing.

Breathe Very Slowly

Now that you're aware of the distinction between a chest and a belly breath, let's focus on ways to establish a relaxed breathing pattern. When you're feeling anxious or experiencing a panic attack, slowing the breath is one of the most important steps you can take to initiate a quieting response.

- Notice the length of each inhalation and exhalation.

- Try evening out the amount of time you spend inhaling and exhaling.

- Pretend you're creating slow, undulating waves, maybe by imagining the gentle rise and fall of waves of water.

- Picture even waves spaced far apart. That's a relaxed pattern.

Counting while inhaling and exhaling can be an effective tool for both remembering to slow down, and balancing the inhalations

STEP 3

with complete exhalations. Remember that hyperventilation occurs when you inhale too much and forget to exhale.

- Inhale to a count of 4 and exhale to a count of 4.

- As you exhale, try letting out the breath through your teeth, creating a soft, hissing sound. Alternatively, exhale as if you were blowing out a candle, blowing away the petals of a dandelion, or moving a toy pinwheel.

- When you're comfortable using a count of 4, inhale to a count of 5 and exhale to a count of 5.

- Now inhale to the count of 4 and exhale to the count of 6.

- Ideally, inhale for 4 seconds (counting one, one thousand, two, one thousand, and so forth) and exhale for 6 seconds (counting in the same manner).

Experiment with Different Breathing Patterns
One of my favorite breathing methods, advocated by Dr. Andrew Weil, produces a profound quieting response.

- Breathe in through your nose as you count slowly to 4.

- Hold your breath as you count to 7.

- Exhale through your mouth as you count to 8.

- Repeat this pattern 4 times in a row and increase to 8 times after you've practiced for a month.

Add Some Images
What if you're taking slow belly breaths, but still feel anxious? What if focusing on breathing makes your more anxious? Rather than give up, keep in mind that the process of change begins with imagination.

STEP 3

- Pretend that slow, abdominal breathing will eventually help you become calmer.

- Imagine the breath sending out signals to your nervous system, telling it to calm down.

- Imagine that the breath is warm and soothing. Go with the image of "soothing" and associate it with something else that feels soothing.

- Imagine the breath moving all the way down to your fingers and toes. Pretend that your fingers and toes are becoming warm and relaxed.

- Imagine a turbulent, stormy sea that will soon become a very calm, smooth body of water, just as your agitated feelings will cease as you create waves of slow, abdominal breaths.

- Imagine the warmth of the breath flowing through your heart. Pretend your chest is "melting" or softening every time you exhale.

- Imagine inhaling feelings of wellbeing.

- Imagine the scary, panicky sensations being exhaled along with the breath.

- Imagine breathing as a child.

- Imagine inhaling equanimity.

- Imagine letting go of any jerkiness in the breath cycle.

- Imagine something that flows, such as flower petals, tall grasses swaying in a gentle breeze or dancers swaying back and forth.

STEP 3

- Say to yourself: "I am" as you inhale and "calm" or "relaxed" as you exhale.

- Say to yourself: "I love" as you inhale, and the name of a favorite person, place, or activity as you exhale.

Another powerful breathing technique involves exhaling into your back body and imagining quieting your adrenal glands. These two "baby" glands sit above the kidneys and secrete the stress hormones associated with the sympathetic response. The surge of adrenaline fuels a panic attack, while cortisol is largely responsible for the feeling of being "keyed up" and on edge.

- Place your hands on your lower back while seated or lying down. As you exhale, imagine your navel moving back towards your spine.

- Picture your breath continuing beyond your spine and puffing out your lower back.

- Imagine your exhaled breath is creating a soft cushion for your adrenal glands or inflating your lower back, as if creating an inner tube.

- Visualize the breath calming and soothing your adrenal glands.

PUTTING TOGETHER STEPS 1 THROUGH 3

Before moving on to Step 4, practice integrating Steps 1, 2, and 3. See yourself letting go of "fearing fear." Remember that the fear response is just your alarm system working well. How about finding some slow, evenly paced belly breaths as you're reading these words? The next time you're feeling anxious, tell yourself that soon your relaxed breaths will turn off the alarm system. Remember that

STEP 3

stopping a panic attack takes time, as the alarm system shuts off gradually. If you don't see a benefit right away, rather than giving up on belly breathing, practice being patient.

Focusing on the breath distracts you from anxiety-producing thoughts. When you create a slow belly breath, for that moment the internal alarm system shuts off. Your autonomic nervous system receives signals indicating the absence of danger; therefore a quieting response begins.

Breath awareness also grounds you in the present moment, an important place to be because anxiety is connected to a future event. Abdominal breathing lays the groundwork for establishing the strong mind–body connection that shuts off a panic reaction. That's why it's my favorite relaxation technique. Slow belly breathing really works!

STEP 3

STEP 4
Let Go of Clenching

UNCLENCH: FINDING MUSCLE RELEASE

Letting go of panic involves loosening up. If you unclench, you'll reach a state of warm wellbeing. Developing positive body awareness, which leads to letting go, first requires recognizing muscle tension. You may not realize that you're chronically bracing, so make awareness the first objective.

Muscles brace in preparation for fighting or running away. What happens if there's no real danger but you're thinking about something scary or wondering if you're about to have a panic attack? Those same muscle groups still brace and tense up because "what's real in the mind is real in the body." Your muscles want to protect you from a physical blow. Due to "muscle memory" you may tighten up without awareness, just finding yourself in similar situations or locations where you experienced anxiety in the past. Whenever you imagine or recall something scary or negative, you tense some muscle somewhere. Notice the muscular sensations that accompany negative thoughts. When muscles tense, they restrict blood circulation and waste energy. Moreover, when the body is tight, so is the mind.

You can shift attention from complete awareness of the panic symptoms to complete attention to the relaxation process. You're already a master at paying attention because you've been doing a wonderful job of immersing yourself in panicking. Wouldn't if be nice to focus completely on the opposite feelings? A great way to stop a panic attack is to find a slow belly breath, then, as you continue this breathing pattern, shift your awareness, your complete attention, to the process of physically letting go of muscle tension.

Become Aware of Clenching

A great method for recognizing muscle tension that's withstood the test of time is progressive muscle relaxation. Originated by Dr. Edmund Jacobson in the 1920s, the technique involves distinguishing between sensations of tension and relaxation while also observing a tendency to hold your breath while clenching. The key to the effectiveness of this practice lies in engaging the mind to discover what's happening in the body. The tighter you tense a muscle, the greater that muscle discharges the tension when you let go. Visualize a pendulum that swings all the way in one direction, then all the way in the other direction when released. Keep this principle in mind as you practice the following exercises in muscle tension awareness:

- Keeping your body still with your arms at your side, bend your right hand back at your wrist as if moving your hand back towards you.

- As you hold this position, notice the tension that spreads to your right forearm. It's easy to feel the strain in your wrist when you flex it back, but what about the less obvious strain in your forearm? Can you feel it in the upper part of the forearm?

- Does your right forearm feel any different than your left forearm? Maybe you notice a dull sensation. That's muscle tension. You may be tightening muscles in this way all day long and not even realize it.

- Now let your right hand rest by your side. How does your right forearm feel now? Do you still experience a dull sensation or does it feel different?

STEP 4

- Observe how your right hand feels when you stop flexing it and let it go limp. That's relaxation! Feel the difference between flexing and letting go.

- With your arms at your sides, make tight fists with both hands. Pretend you're tightly gripping a pencil in each hand. Now release your fists and drop the pencils. Notice the difference between tightness and relaxation.

- Squeeze and release other muscle groups, contrasting the sensations of tension and where it travels, with the sensations of letting go.

Unclench with Slow, Deliberate Movements

Letting go of muscle tension can be either a dynamic or a passive process. Dynamic relaxation, based on the teachings of Dr. Moshe Feldenkrais, involves some type of movement. But this isn't typical movement; it's so slow that you'll barely feel that you're moving. The objective isn't stretching but, rather, relaxing through movement. It's the slow motion process that creates the relaxation effect. Move as if you're "moving through molasses" and make sure to avoid straining. Try these fast and easy ways to unclench using dynamic relaxation:

- Without hiking up your shoulders, very slowly move your right ear towards your right shoulder on a long exhalation.

- Inhale as you lift your head up and then slowly exhale as you repeat on the left side. Notice your neck muscles unclenching.

- Move your shoulders as far forward as you can while inhaling, then upwards towards your ears, then down your back as you exhale.

- Repeat these shoulder circles as often as you like, moving super-slowly. Each time you lower your shoulders away from your ears, enjoy how relaxed your shoulders are becoming.

- While sitting or standing, turn slowly from your waist and gently look behind you while taking a long, slow exhalation.

- Inhale as you come to center and twist to the other side. If sitting, place your left hand just above your right knee to deepen the twist to the right and vice versa. Notice your upper torso unclenching.

Schedule an eye relaxation break to relax and let go of tension. Remember, relaxation has a domino effect; relax a small space and observe how the good feelings spread out and seep into other areas, including the mind. When you relax your eyes and soften the gaze, your mind gets involved observing that process, and ceases to be active.

- Close your eyes and let them sink back into their sockets.

- Take a big belly breath in and, keeping your eyes closed, slowly move your eyes towards the right as you exhale. Take your time, savoring every small movement. Make sure you're not straining by attempting to move too far.

- Inhale and let the smooth breath take your eyes back to the center. Exhale again as you to go to the other side.

- Inhale slowly and then exhale the breath while you move your eyes to the right.

- Draw a big arc with your eyes to move them up and all the way to the left as you take another big abdominal breath.

- Now exhale and take your eyes down and all the way to the right. You're making slow circles, inhaling as you go up and exhaling on the way down. When you tire of going in one direction, switch and move the opposite way.

STEP 4

Unclench by Finding Complete Stillness

Now let's consider some passive relaxation techniques. This process entails letting your muscles go limp by reaching a state of stillness. Trust your body to do what you're telling it to do and imagine you're engaging in self-programming. The formal name for this type of unclenching is autogenic training. Developed by Johannes Schultz in the 1930s, the process typically involves scanning the body from either the crown of the head down to the toes or up from the toes. Repeat each phrase two or three times, pausing for a few seconds in-between to allow the relaxation effect time to take hold. Either record the phrases or have someone guide you if you choose to engage in this process with your eyes closed. Here's the full, unabridged version:

- My scalp is relaxing.

- My hair follicles are relaxing.

- My forehead is smooth.

- The space between my eyebrows is smooth.

- My eyelids are becoming heavy.

- My cheeks are relaxed.

- The edges of my lips are relaxed.

- My lips are relaxed.

- My teeth, my gums and my tongue are relaxed.

- My throat is relaxed.

- My shoulders are loose and relaxed.

- My shoulders are moving away from my ears.

- My upper arms feel heavy and relaxed.

- Heaviness is traveling from my elbow to my forearm.

- My wrists are relaxing.

- My hands, knuckles and fingers are relaxing.

- The tips of my fingers are relaxing.

- The tips of my fingers feel warm and tingly.

- My hands and wrists are relaxing even more.

- Deeper feelings of relaxation are moving back up through my lower arms, elbows, and upper arms.

- My shoulders feel heavy and relaxed.

- My chest muscles are loose and relaxed.

- My stomach muscles are relaxing.

- My pelvis is relaxing.

- My hips are relaxing.

- My thighs are relaxing.

- My knees are softening.

- My lower legs are loose and relaxed.

- My ankles are relaxing.

- The tops of my feet are relaxing.

- My toes are warm and relaxed.

- My toes are tingling with warmth.

- The backs of my feet are relaxed.

- The backs of my ankles are relaxed.

- The backs of my lower legs are relaxed.

STEP 4

- The backs of my knees are relaxed.

- The backs of my thighs are relaxed.

- My buttocks are relaxing.

- The base of my spine is relaxing.

- Warmth is radiating from the base of my spine.

- Relaxing warmth is moving up my spine, vertebrae by vertebrae.

- Relaxing warmth is massaging my back muscles.

- The back of my neck is softening.

- The base of my skull is relaxed.

- The back of my head is relaxed.

- Relaxation is moving to the top of my head.

- My brain is relaxed.

Maybe you're wondering about how these long drawn out muscle relaxation exercises can possibly be helpful if you're in full-blown panic mode. The answer is quite simple. If you focus on unclenching various muscle groups when you're feeling anxious, the mind disengages from the uncomfortable thoughts or sensations. Furthermore, have you ever heard the expression, "An ounce of prevention is worth a pound of cure?" Try releasing physical tension throughout the day and night and you'll be getting a powerful dose of prevention.

Consider the above "script" as a catalogue of possibilities. Perhaps two or three of the autogenic phrases resonated with you. If so, forget about the rest and just repeat these favorites very slowly to yourself, a few times in a row. Maybe you'll trust your creativity and make up your own phrases.

STEP 4

By choosing to practice unclenching when you're already calm and quiet, relaxation deepens and grows stronger. If you practice when you're feeling calm, your brain develops new neural pathways associated with relaxation, so it becomes easier to access these circuits when you start to panic. With practice, muscle relaxation becomes as automatic as the panic response is today. Begin by imagining that this wonderful change will happen. Imagine your brain creating new pathways for calmness. When practicing, notice the feelings of relaxation and tell yourself that you can carry these peaceful feelings with you.

Blend muscle relaxation into your routine in a variety of ways, ranging from mini-sessions to longer, dedicated blocks of time. Welcome any disturbances or conditions that are less than ideal as opportunities to experience the ability to go right back to relaxing. Practice in noisy, crowded places, as that's where panic most often develops. While most relaxation formats come with instructions to close your eyes, it doesn't matter whether your eyes are open or closed. I've seen some clients relax more with their eyes open. It's even possible to engage in the eye relaxation techniques described earlier with your eyes open.

Although many experts recommend practicing for a certain amount of time, typically 20 minutes twice a day, I'm not a proponent of rules for relaxation. Setting up rigid parameters, such as "I have to relax now because this is the time I've set aside for relaxation," can create the anxious state you're attempting to prevent. Simply notice tension and release it, accepting whatever amount of time you direct your attention to the relaxation process. Unclench while sitting, standing, or lying down. As you're reading this sentence, can you turn your attention to a specific muscle group, then squeeze hard and release the tension?

Remember that the mind remains merely the observer along for the ride. That means allowing relaxation to develop at its own pace without expecting a particular result or trying to force the development of a peaceful state.

STEP 4

STRAIGHTEN UP: THE POWER
OF GOOD ALIGNMENT

Muscle relaxation doesn't mean rounding the shoulders and collapsing forward or sinking into an easy chair in a slumped position. Neither produces a relaxation effect; instead, they put strain on the body and make diaphragmatic breathing more difficult. Furthermore, slouching is associated with feeling weak and defeated.

How can good posture have anything to do with stopping a panic attack or lessening anxiety? As you're reading this, hunch over and slouch. Notice how sitting or standing this way lessens the distance between your abdomen and your chest, which makes it harder to take big belly breaths:

- Lift your chest by peeling your bottom ribs away from your diaphragm. Pull your shoulders back and feel your torso lifting away from your hips as you inhale deeply. Imagine growing taller.

- As you straighten up, take a big belly breath again. Notice that you've just created more breathing space.

- Keep lifting your lower ribs, lower your shoulders away from your ears, and lift your chest. Imagine feeling powerful. If you're sitting, notice a feeling of being firmly grounded through your hips. As you feel lifted through your upper body, associate this sensation with growing lighter.

- If you're standing, feel firmly rooted through your feet, like a sturdy tree that has strong roots. No one can knock you over. Imagine a tree with a strong trunk and graceful upper branches. Breathe into this posture.

Keeping the spine straight encourages energy flow and makes it easier to achieve a relaxed state. Standing and sitting tall places the physical body in the best posture for relaxation. Good alignment

STEP 4

also encourages mental relaxation and clarity. Play with the following suggestions:

- Imagine a string reaching from the top of your head to a point in the ceiling. The string is gently holding you up.

- Imagine you're a diva as you feel your torso lifting out of your waist and your spine lengthening.

- Imagine sitting, walking, standing, and breathing in an elegant, regal manner, as if you were a king or queen.

- Imagine you're a ballet dancer with a long neck and straight back.

- Stand like a soldier: relaxed, but at attention.

SLOW DOWN

Are you traveling at a high speed throughout the day? Does rushing lead to racing, which leads to feeling frantic? Mindful movement produces a relaxation response but effort-filled, frantic movements produce stress. Are you talking too fast, eating too fast, or walking too fast to get somewhere? Notice that racing thoughts arise much more easily if you're already racing on a physical level. Just as you want to breathe in slow motion, begin to move more slowly. Experiment with applying the brakes to your rate of speech and walking pace. Maybe you notice that muscles naturally unclench when they're not working so hard.

STEP 4

PUTTING TOGETHER STEPS 1 THROUGH 4

Here's how I combined Steps 1 through 4 to stop a panic attack:

Step 1:

- Chest pain, difficulty breathing, and light-headedness mean I'm experiencing panic.

- I won't fear these sensations.

Step 2:

- I'm not having a heart attack.

- My fearful thoughts set off the alarm system.

- Chest pain, light-headedness, and shortness of breath are part of my body's emergency response to danger.

Step 3:

- Taking slow belly breaths will tell my body to give the "all clear" signal and call off the alarm response.

Step 4:

- Unclenching and enjoying the experience of doing some slow shoulder rolls will send more safety signals to cancel the alarm reaction.

- As I sit tall, I'll wait patiently for the relaxation response to deepen and keep saying to myself, "My chest feels loose and relaxed."

Now practice integrating Steps 1 through 4 using your own unique set of symptoms.

STEP 4

STEP 5
Imagine Something Good

THE POWER OF IMAGINATION

In order for slow abdominal breathing and muscle release to initiate a relaxation response, both mind and body need to be fully engaged in the process of shutting off the alarm system. This process involves imagining "garden hoses" rather than "snakes." Imagining feeling good harnesses so much power that it can even influence the effectiveness of medications. It's called the placebo effect, which has been credited with creating positive changes that can be more powerful than prescription drugs.

Albert Einstein famously stated: "Imagination is more powerful than knowledge." You're not using it to your advantage if you're hyperfocusing on how miserable you feel. When you're stuck in irrational, obsessive thoughts that bring on anxiety and panic, shift to imagining something good. View the process of developing imagery as magical, for the potential exists to experience changes that will be transformational. A vivid imagination shuts the danger signal off and switches the safety signal on.

Remember how you used your imagination as a child? Did you pretend you were a princess or superhero? Did you put on a costume and imagine you were that person? Did you build entire cities from blocks? Did you draw and turn simple shapes into elaborate scenes? Did you make up stories?

During a panic attack you're using the same imaginative powers that you used when you engaged in pretend play. But now you're imagining something negative and the body responds accordingly, so you feel anxious. I bet you'd get an "A+" in imagining the negative and can imagine the worst perfectly. You're probably also great at picturing your limitations, obstacles, past problems, and qualities you believe you're lacking.

By harnessing the imaginative powers that you've been using so well to create a panic response, you can generate a relaxation response. The process of cultivating positive imagery has no guidelines or boundaries. So where to begin? Often the best place to start is far away from the intention to control panic. Just give yourself permission to daydream:

- Imagine somewhere you'd like to be.

- Imagine an event that you'd like attend.

- Imagine something you want to have happen.

- Imagine someone you want to be with.

- Imagine a song you like.

- Imagine the taste of something you like to eat.

- Imagine something good from your childhood.

Try On Relaxation

While the suggestions described above are open-ended and general, it's also possible to get into the habit of imagining a relaxed state. If you consider yourself "an anxious person," imagine characterizing yourself as the polar opposite:

- How would you feel and act if you were relaxed?

- How would you interact with your family and friends?

- How would you behave differently at work or school?

- Where would you travel?

STEP 5

- What new hobbies would you try?

- What new learning would you pursue?

- How would you express your creativity?

- What would wellbeing feel like?

Imagine yourself as relaxed and free of panic attacks:

- If you now think of yourself as a panic attack sufferer or as someone with anxiety, imagine deleting these characterizations.

- Imagine shedding the burden of anxiety the way you would let go of a heavy package that you've been carrying.

- If you've been diagnosed with panic or anxiety disorder, imagine erasing the diagnoses.

- Imagine assuming the mannerisms of someone who's relaxed and easygoing, as if you were an actor playing the part.

- Remember what it was like to pretend? Pretend that you're very relaxed.

- When you start to feel anxious, pretend that you're feeling fine.

The body knows how to relax because it's an innate biological response. You relaxed as an infant and, as a young child, relaxed when you lost yourself in imaginative play. The body can shift to relaxation in the middle of a panic attack. When evoking positive imagery, the judging part of the brain turns off and the body begins to quiet. In this state, you'll find strength, stability, flexibility, and, perhaps most importantly, courage.

STEP 5

Consciously Choose What You Wish to Create

The French psychologist Emile Coué, believed that imagination was much more powerful than willpower. He encouraged his clients to repeat to themselves the famous saying, "Every day, in every way, I am getting better and better." This aphorism may sound corny today, but the underlying message still works: trust in the process of getting better; trust that the mind and body can change:

- Take on the role of a relaxed person in every fiber of your being. What would your shoulders feel like? How would you stand? How would you walk? How would your limbs feel? How would you hold your jaw? How would you breathe? How confident would you feel?

- Can you live your life as if you were better?

- Remember a time when you were extremely relaxed and imagine feeling that way now. How old were you? Where were you at the time? Imagine the sights, sounds, smells, and textures that surrounded you. Pretend you're there now.

If you're thinking to yourself, "I can't think of a time when I was relaxed" or "there was never a time when I didn't feel anxious," these thoughts move your entire being into the danger zone and turn on the alarm system. A more accurate statement would be, "I haven't been anxious 100 percent of the time, every single waking and sleeping moment of my life." Now you've awakened to the possibility of remembering some peaceful feelings.

Another strategy consists of adding images to contrast panic and relaxation:

- Imagine pushing your panic away. Give it a shape and color and imagine it moving farther and farther away, getting smaller and smaller.

STEP 5

- Imagine a shape and color for relaxation. Imagine the shape and color of the panic changing to the shape and color of relaxation, which is coming closer and closer to you.

- Imagine bright lights. Assign panic the color red and choose green for relaxation. Imagine the lights changing from red to purple to blue and finally to a beautiful shade of green.

THE POWER OF DAYDREAMING

When the mind creates a movie of a favorite place or experience, mental contentment and physical relaxation soon follow because "what's real in the mind is real in the body." Use the suggestions below to create your own collection of images.

Imagine Somewhere Outdoors

Connecting with nature is one of the most popular ways to create a relaxation response. As the senses awaken, joyful feelings typically emerge. When the heart and mind are busy experiencing a sense of wonder, there's no space for anxiety. Consider again that "what's real in the mind is real in the body." If you recreate a magnificent vista, for example, your body responds as if you're actually there at that very moment in time.

Paint a mental picture of your favorite settings. What natural surroundings do you associate with joy and serenity? Photographs and paintings of beautiful landscapes can serve as taking-off points for imagining being in these locations right now. Find a scene that you like and step into it with full sensory awareness; for example:

- a brilliant sunrise or sunset

- a favorite beach

STEP 5

- a forest of towering pine trees

- the top of a mountain

- a flowering garden.

Now enrich these images. The mind can begin with one comforting image and travel on as one association leads to another:

- How about a sunrise or sunset over a lake? Can you see the stillness of the water? What sounds can you hear in the distance? Can you feel a gentle breeze across your face?

- Imagine lying on a beautiful beach. Can you feel the sand beneath you and hear the sounds of the ocean? Can you picture the waves and imagine your breath is creating that same wave pattern?

- How about following a butterfly through a garden? Is it sunny outside? Picture the garden awakening. Can you zoom in and see colors? Focus on one flower and watch it sway in the light breeze. Add a bird's song.

- Take an imaginary nature walk and let it be a sensory experience. Look at the sky; notice the sun filtering through the trees. Observe the various colors of the leaves and the shape of tree limbs. Feel the firmness of the earth beneath your feet, the breeze touching your skin. Imagine feeling pure joy as you notice signs of life all around.

- Pretend you're drifting on a canoe in calm waters. Experience the stillness of the surroundings. Imagine recreating that stillness within you at this moment.

- Take in the sights, sounds and smells of a meadow. Now stand on a hill overlooking the meadow.

STEP 5

- Imagine arriving at the top of a tall mountain. Take in the magnificent vista that surrounds you. Lift your arms up to the sky and feel complete joy. Imagine being filled up with that power.

- If you're in the mood for a different season, imagine walking in newly fallen snow. Observe the white world that surrounds you. See the tracks you're creating. Feel the stillness, the quiet that surrounds you, and imagine recreating that inside you right now. Make snow angels. Build a snowman or a fort. See yourself laughing and being silly. See yourself as strong and invincible.

Can you step into this "outdoor cathedral"?
Photo courtesy of Dorothy Zeviar

STEP 5

Imagine Welcoming Indoor Places

Maybe you don't enjoy being outdoors. Instead, imagine the following scenes coming alive, as if you were creating a movie:

- Imagine sitting inside and taking in a wonderful vista.

- Imagine watching snow falling.

- Imagine the sound of rain on the roof while you're safe and warm inside.

- Imagine looking out and seeing the most brilliant display of fall colors.

- Imagine observing the movement of the clouds.

- Imagine trees or flowers outside your window.

- Imagine sitting beside a window and basking in a pool of sunlight on a cold, wintery day.

As an alternative to the marvels of nature, move to an interior view instead:

- Picture your childhood room.

- Recreate the kitchen of your childhood home.

- Imagine a roaring fireplace.

- Visualize a beautiful bathroom with an inviting bathtub.

- Envision a cozy nook for reading.

- Imagine watching a burning candle or an array of candles of all shapes and sizes.

Once the location is established, let your imagination go and fill in the details:

- If you like remembering your childhood room, can you fill the room with your favorite toys? What did cuddling in your bed under your blanket feel like? Do you want to turn on your favorite music from that time period? Can you imagine the texture of your pillow, the scent? Can you see the color and feel the texture of the comforter or blanket on your bed?

- Can you imagine the smell of soup cooking on the stove providing satisfying nourishment on a cold, rainy day? Can you imagine the aroma of bread baking in the oven? Are there other aromatic pleasures that you want to surround yourself with? Do you want to imagine being served a wonderful meal at a beautifully set table that has been prepared just for you?

- Can you imagine sitting by the fireplace? Do you feel warmth emanating from the fire? Can you hear the crackling of the logs? Can you watch the dancing of the flames?

- Can you feel the water as you lean back and soak in the tub? Do you want to add an essential oil? How about candles? Do you want scented candles? Would music add something special to the scene? Feel the warmth and pretend it's enveloping you right now. Imagine your skin softening. Pretend that you're warming and softening on the inside as well.

- Imagine growing something or planting an indoor herb garden. What herbs come to mind? Breathe in their scents.

- How about pretending that you're gathering some chamomile, mint, lemon balm, or lavender (calming herbs you'll learn about in Step 9)? Fresh from your imaginary garden, place them into a tea ball and make a pot of tea. Inhale the steam from the tea. Feel soothed. Maybe you

STEP 5

prefer smelling fresh basil or rosemary? Where does your imagination go now?

Imagine Pleasurable Activities

Can you take any activity that gives you pleasure and picture yourself enjoying this experience right now? Imagine moving from one to another. Consider the following possibilities, but, more importantly, create your own.

- Getting a wonderful massage.
- Swimming.
- Floating on a raft in a beautiful pool.
- Riding a bicycle.
- Playing cards.
- Listening to a symphony.
- Playing golf.
- Doing yoga.
- Hiking.
- Playing basketball.
- Jogging.
- Dancing.
- Hula-hooping.

STEP 5

The Joy of Hooping

ADD SOMEONE SPECIAL

Nature's wonders can fill us with awe and help create stillness in mind and body, as can imagining indoor places and favorite activities, but imagining favorite people or pets takes the relaxation response to a deeper level because the heart engages:

- Take any of the fantasy trips you created above and add someone special to the scene. Add a whole group of people.

- Simply imagine the faces of people you love, as if you were viewing a slideshow.

- Imagine holding a baby against your chest. Feel her warmth and softness. Notice her sweet smells. Imagine her warmth penetrating and warming your chest.

- Imagine holding hands or embracing a special person in your life.

STEP 5

- Imagine your pet resting on your lap. Notice the warmth of his body. Stroke his fur. Feel his breathing.

I remember being called in to see a hospitalized patient who was diagnosed with metastatic cancer and experiencing anxiety and pain. I led her through an abdominal breathing process and she immediately associated images of warmth with having her beloved cat resting peacefully on her belly. As she closed her eyes, she felt the warmth from her cat soothing her both physically and emotionally. This image also helped her maintain abdominal breathing.

Create Your Own Scripts

Although the best creative imagining occurs spontaneously, you may want something ready made that can guide you into a relaxed state.

- Picture a scene where you're comfortable, safe, and relaxed, a place where you can leave the outside pressures and demands behind.

- Imagine yourself in some location where you were relaxed in the past, or create an image of your ideal vacation or fantasy trip. Make your mental movie come alive by using all your senses.

A popular guided visualization takes you to the beach:

- Imagine descending a long staircase and finding yourself at a beautiful beach. Observe the color of the water, see the horizon in the distance, hear the sound of the waves and the seagulls flying over the ocean, feel the sand between your toes. Find a comfortable chair, put down your belongings, and settle in as you close your eyes and bask in the warming rays of the sun.

A path in the woods or leading up to a mountain offers many possibilities for creative imagery:

STEP 5

- As you walk along, see the tall trees, smell the ground beneath you, the smell of earth. Notice the colors of any wildflowers beside the path. See the blue sky through the treetops. Hear rushing water off in the distance. Come to a mountain stream or a waterfall. Pause to take in your surroundings: the sights, the smells, and the sounds. Continue walking along the path until you arrive at the top of a hill. What do you see as you look out over the hill? This can be your special place to relax.

Create a few scripts by closing your eyes, painting a wonderful mental picture, and bringing it to life. Record it on the voice memo application on your phone or write it down. If you trust in the power of your imagination, these scripts will be as effective at stopping an anxiety attack as the pill that so many people carry with them "just in case."

IMAGINING WITH YOUR BREATH

Positive imagery and relaxed breathing go hand in hand. As you know by now, breathing creates the foundation for wellbeing, but blending creative imagery with breathing strengthens and deepens this process. You began merging breathing with imagery in Step 3; now you'll practice going further to enhance the relaxation effect:

- As you push out your belly to take in a breath, turn your attention to the air just outside your nostrils. Notice how it feels.

- Can you imagine the air tickling your nose? Is it rushing in like a strong gust of wind? Can you slow it down until it becomes a gentle breeze coming through an open window?

- Notice the temperature of the air you inhale. Does it feel cool?

STEP 5

Feeling warm or overheated is common during or just before a panic attack, so imagine inhaling cool, refreshing air.

- Associate cool air with that good feeling of stepping into a cool place when you're hot.

- Pretend there's a cool breeze coming in from an open window.

- Imagine the movement of air from an overhead circulating fan.

- Imagine walking by the ocean enjoying the clean, cool fresh air.

What about the opposite? What's it like to imagine the warmth of the breath? We usually associate warmth with something soothing.

- As you exhale by pulling your navel towards your spine, imagine that your body has warmed the air you inhaled.

- Imagine that your belly is a furnace that's warming the air you've taken in. Feel the soothing warmth of the breath flow through you.

- Imagine feeling comfortably warm, experiencing the warmth of snuggling under a cozy blanket when it's cold outside.

- Imagine warm oil on your skin or the feeling of warm hands when getting a massage.

- Imagine being on a beautiful beach and walking on warm sand.

- Imagine your breath as creating a warm inner glow.

STEP 5

- As you draw in air, imagine inhaling something warm and calming. As you exhale, imagine this warm, soothing substance spreading from head to toe.

In with the Good, Out with the Bad

Functional medicine boils down to putting what's good into your body, such as healing foods, and removing what's bad, such as sugar-laden processed foods. Viewed more broadly, it's also about putting in good thoughts and emotions and letting go of negative ones. From mind-body medicinal research, we know the healing power of letting in something good and letting go of something bad through the endless possibilities of using your imagination.

- Imagine what you need right now and inhale it with the next breath. Imagine what you want to get rid of and exhale it along with the stale air.

- Imagine inhaling feelings of peacefulness. Imagine exhaling little bits of the panicky feeling.

Any sensation that feels good can be breathed into the body, including joy, lightness, steadiness, balance, calmness, strength, flexibility, warmth, coolness, or a complete sense of equanimity.

- As you inhale with your belly, draw in full deep breaths of joy. Imagine joy coming into every pore on your skin, as if your skin was one big breathing organ.

- As you inhale, breathe in feelings of lightness in your belly and your upper body, as if you're lifting a heavy burden off your chest and creating more breathing space. As you exhale, feel grounded and a sense of steadiness through your lower body, as if you're firmly planted or rooted.

STEP 5

➤ With each breath, imagine the feeling of equanimity growing stronger. Stay with the feeling. It will dissolve after a few seconds. Go back to your breath and feel it again.

Imagine Breathing through the Heart

When the mind, the breath, and the heart create harmony, then you experience peacefulness. Let's explore how we can harness the power of the heart. While medical textbooks describe the heart in terms of its physiological function, our emotional sense of the heart is quite different. Rather than simply pumping blood, the heart plays a central role in how we think and feel. Positive feelings in the heart create a ripple effect that sends wellbeing throughout the body. You can access its intelligence and power to lead you to a calm state of awareness.

Dating back thousands of years, yogi masters, poets, and philosophers have referred to the heart as the center of life, the internal "guru." Science now confirms that the heart has its own brain and nervous system, which relays information back to the brain, creating a two-way communication process. Heartbeats are actually an intelligent language, as these rhythmic beating patterns are transformed into neural impulses that directly affect the higher brain centers. More specifically, as the heart beat changes, so does electrical activity in the amygdala, the part of the brain responsible for processing emotions.

Heart rate variability patterns, the measurements of the beat-to-beat changes in heart rate, also referred to as heart rhythms, are powerful direct reflections of our inner emotional state. Increasing heart rate variability reduces the activity of the sympathetic nervous system and increases the activity of the parasympathetic branch. By accessing feelings such as compassion, appreciation, and forgiveness, heart rate variability increases, rhythmical breathing ensues, and the parasympathetic branch keeps the stress response in check. In other words, you're keeping the brake on (the parasympathetic response) to prevent the alarm from going off (the sympathetic response).

Breathing patterns influence heart rhythms and vice versa, as the heart is the primary regulator of respiratory rhythm. How does this happen? The answer lies in the experience of positive emotions, sincerely feeling love, care, and gratitude:

- Imagine your breath flowing through your heart.

- Imagine the warmth of the breath warming your heart.

- Imagine feeling grateful for someone or something in your life or recall a positive feeling or time and re-experience that feeling at this moment.

- Become aware of a warm, melting sensation right in the center of your chest.

The mind doesn't calm the mind, the heart does. So focus on your heart as if it were the center of your being. Remember to evoke positive emotions, the crucial ingredients that warm the heart and calm the mind.

Purposely slowing down your belly breathing can be a good place to begin breathing through the heart. Focus on slowing your breath to about 6 breaths per minute or 10 seconds per breath, as you learned in Step 3. As you take 6 breaths per minute, imagine the warmth of the breath warming and soothing your heart.

We associate a warm heart with warm emotions. Where your mind travels to when imagining feelings of gratitude doesn't matter as long as positive emotions are generated. Think of the heart as moving from being a closed fist to an extended open hand. Imagine the heart as big, open, and smiling.

Getting more specific usually creates more intense feelings of love and gratitude. For example, as you imagine warm breath flowing in and out of your heart, imagine the feeling of looking into the eyes of a loved one and having that person look back at you. My heart warms

STEP 5

instantly whenever I imagine the smiling faces of my daughters when they were small children. The heart keeps the break on the stress response when it opens and fills with love. Similarly, imagine the feeling in your chest when someone gives you a hug, maybe after you've had a fight and forgiven each other, and your heart fills with gratitude. To deepen the experience, try placing your right hand over your heart. Imagine warm feelings radiating in concentric circles from your heart. Don't forget to incorporate feelings of self-love.

If you practice warming your heart in response to everyday annoyances and disappointments, you'll establish a memory bank of success stories; solid evidence that in just a short period of time your physical and emotional state can be dramatically altered. By practicing on petty frustrations, you'll be prepared to breathe into your heart center if panic signals emerge.

Just feel gratitude for anything at all and the heart will know what to do with that emotion. What can you find to appreciate when starting to panic? Can you appreciate that your alarm system works so well? Can you feel grateful to still be standing? Can you marvel at how efficiently the mind produces so many negative thoughts in such a short period of time?

The heart's signals influence those around us. Negativity or fear produces a different signal to appreciation. The resulting energy radiates beyond the physical body. How many times have you felt either comfortable or uneasy around someone but may not have been able to fully articulate why? Have you heard of the expression "giving off negative vibes"? Thoughts and feelings have their own magnetic energy that attracts energy of a similar nature. So negative energy attracts negative energy and positive energy attracts positive energy. Try warming your heart by finding gratitude the next time you're with someone who's negative.

The powerful heart warming techniques I've been describing come from research conducted by the Institute for HeartMath. I highly recommend purchasing either the Emwave Personal Stress Reliever or Inner Balance (a device that attaches to a smartphone).

STEP 5

These portable trainers provide immediate feedback and guide you towards finding a slow breath cycle and increasing heart rate variability. Find the links through my website: www.heartmath.org.

One note of caution: since panic is frequently associated with a racing, pounding heart, often the mere mention of the word "heart" may lead you down the path towards a full-blown panic attack. Overly focused on micromanaging physical functions, you may spend a considerable amount of time listening to your heart beating or vigilantly watching for chest pains. If this is the case, you're not ready to focus attention on the beating of the heart or imagine the breath flowing through the heart. Instead, take some slow belly breaths, picture someone or something you're grateful for, and imagine one of the happiest days of your life.

THE POWER OF LOVING KINDNESS

Invoking feelings of love and kindness brings about the same healing benefits as warming the heart through gratitude. Try this loving kindness exercise, popularized by Jon Kabat-Zinn, the developer of the Mindfulness Based Stress Reduction Program at the University of Massachusetts Medical Center.

Begin by saying to yourself:

- May I be filled with loving kindness.

- May I be peaceful and at ease.

- May I be happy.

Proceed to extending warm wishes to someone close to you. Visualize that person as you say to yourself:

- May you be free from suffering.

- May you be happy and at ease.

STEP 5

Picture as many people as you like: immediate family, extended family, friends, acquaintances, and even someone you have a difficult time getting along with or whose presence evokes an anxiety reaction. Feel free to spread feelings of loving kindness to everyone who suffers, or to all beings on the planet. Implicit in a loving kindness practice is the letting go of negative emotions and an acceptance of "what is" at this given moment. On a physical level, this practice leads to a profound relaxation response.

KEEP A SUPPLY OF POSITIVE IMAGES HANDY

Even though the best associations occur spontaneously, tangible reminders can come in handy, so have positive images easily accessible to you. In the midst of a full-blown panic attack, evoking helpful imagery can be challenging as the symptoms of panic take center stage and it's difficult to focus on anything but the awful feelings of anxiety:

- Post pictures that evoke positive associations in easily viewable locations, such as bathroom mirrors, by the kitchen sink, and on electronic devices.

- Carry a picture with you combined with a verbal description to be read aloud when you're beginning to feel uncomfortable.

- Prepare relaxing images in advance, similar to rehearsing a speech.

- Create a slideshow of soothing images on your computer or cell phone.

- Write an appreciation list as entries in a journal, a recording device or even a memo application on a computer or cell phone.

STEP 5

My screensaver image of Buddha, the ocean, and Hawaii: sheer bliss

As you practice imagining something good, pretty soon you'll have a very powerful image to use: the memory of stopping panic. You can think back to this breakthrough experience and remember it when symptoms develop. Your memory bank will expand as more of these panic-stopping episodes accumulate.

PUTTING TOGETHER STEPS 1 THROUGH 5

Step 1:

- Choose not to "fear fear."

Step 2:

- Tell yourself that negative thoughts or images switched on your alarm system.

Step 3:

- Find some slow, evenly paced belly breaths.

STEP 5

- Tell yourself that soon your relaxed breaths will turn off the alarm system.

Step 4:

- Notice if you're tightening up, slouching, or moving too fast.

- Purposefully unclench, straighten up, and slow down your movements.

Step 5:

- Imagine letting in something good and letting out what's bad.

- Let your imagination take you to a wonderful, relaxing place.

- Imagine the warmth of your breath circulating through your heart and let your heart open to love and gratitude.

STEP 5

STEP 6
Think Rationally

Turning your attention to breathing, positive imagery, and muscle relaxation provides a distraction from anxiety-producing thoughts. Now we're going to confront that inner voice head on so you can eliminate irrational thoughts and stop the mental storm. Irrational thinking is either totally out of step with reality or consists of unnecessary exaggeration. You disturb yourself from the way you talk to yourself about your problems, not from the problems themselves.

Negative self-talk is usually a replay of old scripts you've had all your life. Often it's filled with self-defeating lines such as "I'm not going to be able to do this." You're going to learn how to delete statements like this and, instead, think rationally, like a scientist.

People don't make you angry. Situations don't make you depressed or fearful. Bodily sensations don't cause panic. The way you think about these experiences causes the negative reactions. The event can't get inside your physical body and turn on the stress response. If you believe that a particular person or situation makes you anxious, that's like believing that the garden hose, rather than the thought of a snake, created the panic reaction I described in Step 2.

PLAY THE DETECTIVE

To begin, let's analyze an experience that might be anxiety-provoking and identify the accompanying self-talk that could trigger the alarm system. Imagine giving a speech in front of a large audience. If this prospect scares you, chances are your self-talk includes the words "what if," as in "What if I forget what I want to say?" or "What if I start to feel anxious during the talk?" How about "have to" or "must," as in "I have to do a good job" or "I must not embarrass myself"? Consider these words the "snakes" that turn on the alarm system.

Consider the following symptoms:

- chest tightness

- heart beating quickly

- dizziness

- sweating

- nausea.

What interpretations might follow?

- "I'm feeling horrible!"

- "I have to get out of here!"

- "Something is really wrong with me!"

- "I must be having a heart attack!"

- "I'm going to pass out!"

A panic attack might be the consequence of these interpretations. Play the detective and practice identifying the following common reasoning flaws in your own self-talk or dialogue with others:

Are You Catastrophizing?

- You imagine the worst.

- You frequently use the word "awful" when describing how you feel.

- You often say, "it's terrible" or "it's horrible."

Magnifying, or blowing something up way beyond proportion, means you're catastrophizing. Keep up this type of crazy self-talk and you're creating anxiety and on the way to a full-blown panic attack.

Are You Overgeneralizing?

- You often use the word "always."

- "Never" comprises a big part of your self-talk or your conversations with others.

When you engage in all-or-nothing thinking and see things in black or white categories, you're producing anxiety.

Is Your Mental Filter Broken?

- You zoom in on a single negative detail.

- You stay focused on the negative.

If you're dwelling on the negative, your vision of all reality becomes obscured.

Do You Minimize or Disqualify the Positive?

- You say, "yes, but" a lot.

Do you reject positive experiences or sensations by insisting they don't count?

STEP 6

Do You Jump to Conclusions?

- You frequently jump to negative conclusions.

- You predict that situations will turn out badly.

This reasoning error involves interpreting events negatively without definite facts to support your conclusion. You're engaging in mind-reading: predicting that situations will turn out badly. Consider a career as a fortune teller.

Emotional Reasoning

The irrational assumption that your negative emotions reflect reality underlies all of the thinking flaws mentioned above.

THE POWER OF HOT WORDS

Irrational thoughts typically contain specific buzzwords. Search for them, as the mind races so quickly that they may be difficult to catch. Sometimes they're not clearly articulated, but embedded in mental images. How frequently do you use the following "hot words"?

- should

- must

- have to

- always

- never

- can't

- nothing.

STEP 6

Do you have a strongly held view about how you "should" be or how you "should" or "shouldn't" feel?

- "I shouldn't be feeling this way."

- "I should be comfortable and panic-free at all times."

- "I should be able to control these panicky feelings."

What may underlie these statements is the irrational premise: "I must be in control at all times." The need to be in control requires an extreme amount of effort and energy. Because it's such hard work to maintain this state, the stress response may be in overdrive.

Are you detecting a lot of "always" or "nevers"?

- "I'll never be able to change."

- "I always get nervous in these situations."

What's the impact of "can't"?

- "I can't stand feeling this way."

- "I can't breathe with my belly."

- "I can't relax."

- "I can't change."

What about the power of "nothing"?

- "Nothing will stop these panic attacks."

- "Nothing is helping."

- "Nothing I do to relax makes a difference."

STEP 6

BECOME A SCIENTIST

Thinking scientifically means challenging and disputing irrational thinking. By attacking the "hot words" you introduce realistic thinking. Simply replace the negative mind chatter with more positive ideas and overcome fears by challenging irrational beliefs.

"It's No Big Deal!"

Watch for the tendency to turn everything into a "big deal." Many situations that seem to be very important at the time they're happening are no big deal the next day or the following week. Are you upset today about something that will be soon forgotten?

- Can you remember what you worried about in high school?

- Do you have a memory of fretting over a particular grade on a test?

- Can you recall the times you panicked about being late for an appointment?

- Can you remember panicking because you misplaced or lost something?

- Do you remember feeling upset because you damaged your car?

How much impact have these incidents really had on your life?

"So What If...?"

If I had to chose one technique for quieting the mind, turning "what ifs" into "so what ifs" wins hands down. "What if" implies trying to predict and therefore control an impending catastrophe. Saying "so what if" implies giving up the mental picture of future doom and gloom and therein resides the power of this statement.

STEP 6

By catching "what ifs" and adding a "so," danger signals morph into safety signals and the alarm system deactivates.

- So what if I'm late? It happened before and it turned out to be no big deal.

- So what if I fail this test? I'll survive.

- So what if I screw up this speech? It won't matter in ten years.

- So what if my heart's beating fast? I've experienced this before and it slowed down.

- So what if I'm sweating? My sweat glands are doing their job to keep me cool.

- So what if I have a panic attack? I won't die from it or go crazy.

Practice turning these catastrophic questions into "so what ifs":

- What if I start to shake?

- What if I get anxious and start to panic while giving a speech?

- What if I feel a panic attack coming on while attending a meeting?

- What if I choose to leave?

- What if someone notices that I'm leaving?

- What if I start to panic and I'm alone in the house?

- What if I get scared while driving?

- What if they criticize me?

STEP 6

- What if I'm away from home and I feel sick?

- What if I'm alone and scared and it's the middle of the night?

- What if I get anxious while sitting in a theater?

- What if my boss doesn't like my work?

- What if my panic upsets others?

- What if my kids see me having a panic attack?

- What if someone says something that upsets me?

- What if I have a setback?

- What if I need medication?

- What if I never overcome panic?

By putting a "so" in front you're imagining coping with a future scary possibility and quieting the mind, which turns off the alarm system in the present moment. Additionally, you're rehearsing a coping strategy if the scenario you're saying "what if?" about were actually to occur at some point in the future. That's what makes this strategy so effective.

Add a Back-up Plan to the "So What Ifs"

What's more anxiety-relieving than picturing a "way out"? Say to yourself, "So what if...? I can always..." For example, if you're anxious in anticipation of attending an event with large crowds of people, imagine leaving. Most importantly, imagine taking this action without rating yourself a failure. Just thinking of an escape route prevents worrisome thoughts from getting out of control.

STEP 6

Find Positive "What Ifs" for a Change

Accustomed to the negative "what ifs," how often do you find positive "what ifs"?

- What if I become relaxed?

- What if belly breathing stops a panic attack?

- What if I take a chance?

- What if I feel better?

Imagine Coping with the Worst

If you're skilled at imagining the worst, add a coping resource. Pick any fear-producing situation or remember a time when you had a panic attack. Imagine, as vividly as you can, how you would tolerate the fear and the physical sensations that accompany it. Saying "not a big deal" entails imagining the worst, then imagining coping with it, maybe even enjoying the outcome.

- Imagine you're late for an important meeting.

- What's the worst thing that can happen? Maybe someone will notice your tardiness.

- What's the worst that can happen then? Maybe you'll give a bad impression or get a negative review.

- What's the worst that can happen from a negative review? Maybe you'll get fired.

- What's the worst that can happen if you lose your job? That would be bad, but would it be life-threatening?

- Is it possible that getting fired could even lead to a better future? Picture one door closing, but another opening.

STEP 6

- Now go back to the realistic consequences of being late. What are the odds that it's "not a big deal" and you wouldn't actually lose your job?

Think like Dr. Spock

On *Star Trek*, a television show first popular in the 1960s, and later made into a series of motion pictures, Dr. Spock, one of the principal characters, was completely rational, never letting emotions get in the way of judgment because he was incapable of processing emotions. To counter the fear-producing inner voice, become Dr. Spock. Think like a scientist who performs an experiment free from bias.

Your brain is critical, judgmental, and anything but objective. Interpretations are merely guesses, not scientific facts. Your beliefs represent one of several possible hypotheses and tend to be biased. So cultivate a scientific brain and challenge biased thinking:

- Think of five things you worried about in the past week.

- How many actually happened?

Just the Facts, Ma'am

On *Dragnet*, a television program that aired in the 1950s, Sergeant Joe Friday famously told his witnesses, "Just the facts, ma'am." Do the facts of the situation back up what you think? Are any of the following catastrophic declarations actually facts?

- I can't stand it.

- I'm going to fail.

- I'll never get over this.

- I can't relax.

Will It Hold up in a Court of Law?

When I hear irrational statements, I often ask clients to imagine they're on a witness stand. Would this statement hold up in a courtroom or would it be dismissed as conjecture? Where is the evidence, the indisputable facts? Can you find an alternative view? Find as many alternatives as you can. When you consider the facts objectively, which alternative is most likely to be correct? There are many different ways to look at any experience. How else can you interpret what's happening? The process might look something like this:

- Where's the proof that these physical sensations mean I'm having a heart attack?

- So I have chest pain. What else could be causing that? Can chest pain come from tightening my muscles?

- Can chest pain indicate muscle soreness?

- Is it possible that I tightened up due to anxiety and interpreted the resulting chest pains as a sure sign of a heart attack?

Where's the Evidence?

Challenge your assumptions by asking one of my favorite questions: "Where's the evidence?"

- Where's the evidence that I can't relax?

- How do I know that?

- Am I 100 percent certain?

- Have I ever learned something in the past?

STEP 6

- Am I concluding beforehand that I can't master these skills?

- Is it possible that my body knows how to relax but my interfering mind gets in the way?

- Does thinking this way help or hurt me?

Is It Happening Right Now?

Anxious thoughts falsely assume something about the future, while fear of what might imminently occur defines a panic response. Stopping panic and quieting an anxious mind means stepping out of the time machine and returning to the present. Ask yourself, "What tense am I in?" Knowing a future outcome in advance, such as failure or panic, requires the magic powers of a fortune teller.

- If you're so skilled at seeing into the future, maybe you have super powers the rest of us mere mortals don't possess.

- With this ability to know what will happen next, you could be making millions in the stock market or betting in Las Vegas.

Easing the mind means deleting the "what might be" prediction.

- The future isn't here yet, so focus awareness on "what is."

- Where's the evidence that something bad is happening at this very moment in time?

What's the best way to stay anchored in the present moment? Come back to your breath, unclench, and notice with all your senses what surrounds you.

STEP 6

GETTING COMFORTABLE WITH UNCOMFORTABLE FEELINGS

They're Just Sensations

If you're prone to panic, you're probably tuning in to physical sensations much more than your calm and carefree friend or colleague. Imagine two people standing in a hot, crowded room. They both feel warm and begin to sweat. The first woman says to herself, "It's hot in here; I'll feel better when I step outside." The other says to herself, "I'm not feeling well; I'm sweating; it's getting difficult to breathe; I feel as if I could pass out; what if I faint?" The second example exemplifies the self-talk of someone on her way to a panic attack. What's the difference? The first woman observed the uncomfortable sensations, but interpreted them as normal and temporary. Although harmless physical fluctuations occur for many reasons, such as changes in hormonal levels or biological rhythms, panic-sufferers forget that these sensations are perfectly normal. Are you overreacting to normal fluctuations and proceeding to scare yourself over these sensations?

Which normal sensations might be misinterpreted?

+ Breathlessness from physical exercise.

+ Increased heart rate from physical exercise.

+ Nausea from overeating.

+ Fullness or bloating after a heavy meal.

+ Disorientation from consuming alcohol or cannabis.

+ Getting overheated on a warm day.

+ Fatigue from lack of sleep.

+ Hunger.

+ Thirst.

STEP 6

- Muscle tension due to frustration, anger or other strong emotions.

- Sweating.

A huge step in conquering panic is accepting bodily sensations as is, without interpreting them as dangerous or leading to a serious condition.

But I Panic in the Middle of the Night

- My panic attacks can't be related to thoughts or breathing patterns because I wake up in the middle of the night with panic.

- So they have to just happen by themselves, right?

Wrong. Although it may appear as though the panic is coming out of nowhere, in fact it's related to subtle cues. Fluctuations in physiological rhythms during the night are perfectly normal. Heart rate and respiration increase at times, especially if you go to bed with a lot on your mind or in an anxious state. If these fluctuations occur with an increase in level of consciousness, such as between sleep stages, then you may awaken with full-blown panic, referred to as a nocturnal panic attack. If you're sensitive to, and frightened by, sensations, it's understandable that these changes, combined with the disorientation of waking, could lead to a panic reaction. In fact, many people awaken from sleep in a panic.

When Relaxation Leads to Panic

- Relaxation doesn't work for me.

- It just makes me more anxious.

STEP 6

If you experience anxiety due to a relaxed state, you're not alone. Deep relaxation may be a novel experience and letting go may be associated with sudden fear, possibly related to a perceived loss of control. Relaxation often involves body scanning and observing physical sensations, which might not be recognized if attention was focused on thoughts or external events. The mind misinterprets normal bodily sensations that stem from the relaxation response. Once again, fear arises in reaction to a reasoning error, in this instance, jumping to false conclusions about feelings associated with letting go.

PRACTICE, BUT EXPECT TO DO SO IMPERFECTLY

Consider the mind to be like putty. Now picture that putty being reshaped as you practice changing irrational thoughts to rational ones. There's exciting new evidence that patterns of thinking actually change brain structure and function. By practicing new learning over and over again, the body changes and the mind responds. Of all the many complex tasks you mastered, weren't they all done badly at first? Even when you noticed some improvement, you still made mistakes, but they occurred less frequently because you kept practicing. Mastery comes through practice, so just start collecting those practice hours. Begin by taking a chance. What opportunities exist to practice coping with fears? You can schedule a rehearsal and also take advantage of the actual "performance" as practice time.

Rehearse, then Rehearse Some More

Theater companies wouldn't consider mounting a production without scheduling rehearsals. Olympic athletes train for the big event. Law students rehearse in moot courts. Police and fire departments rehearse for emergencies. How can rehearsal work for

STEP 6

panic? Just like getting ready for a performance, you're programming yourself now to be relaxed later.

By rehearsing, you're giving yourself a stress inoculation. After receiving a vaccine inoculation, the body produces antibodies to prevent a disease. Stress inoculation, based on the work of Donald Michenbaum, works the same way as it involves preparation for coping with impending danger. A moderate amount of anxiety results from imagining a stressful situation. By imagining the situation over and over again, the anxiety gradually lessens. By rehearsing the dreaded event so often, you become familiar with it and rob it of its danger.

But Isn't the Problem Imagining Stressful Events?

Yes, you're a master at anticipating and reliving the scary situation, but you're focusing on the negative. With stress inoculation, imagine the fear-producing event and simultaneously rehearse coping skills. We're throwing out the old script and rehearsing a new version. The new script is filled with rational self-statements combined with positive imagery and slow, steady breathing.

It may seem unnatural and forced to search for your thoughts, challenge them, and then find a rational alternative. Remember, you're learning a new skill, and just as with breathing, unclenching, and the use of imagery, as you practice you'll soon be thinking scientifically. The key word is practice.

Try memorizing a simple monologue while rehearsing. It can go something like this:

- I'm going to be fine.

- I've succeeded with this before.

- Soon it'll be over.

- If I get anxious, it's a cue to find my breath.

- It's just a sensation.

- I can patiently wait for my body to relax.

Enhance your rehearsal by adding contingency plans. Imagine going to a performance but you're afraid you'll have a panic episode while trapped in the middle of the row. Rehearse with imagery, breathing, unclenching muscles, and self-talk. Add the back-up plan, "I can leave." If you're thinking, "But what if I can't leave?" or "It would be too embarrassing," rehearse saying "What a perfect opportunity to practice letting go of embarrassment or shame." What's the worst that would happen if you left your seat? Have you ever been at a theater, church, sports stadium, and noticed someone leave their seat? How many reasons could you think of as to why he or she left? Did you pay more than passing attention?

Combine your imaginative powers with your rational voice as you rehearse for the live performance. Rehearsal boosts self-confidence, offers hope and increases the perceived sense of control. By counteracting feelings of helplessness, a successful practice run promotes the expectation that positive changes will happen.

PANIC: AN OPPORTUNITY TO PRACTICE

If symptoms of panic develop, use the occasion as an opportunity to practice what you've rehearsed. Opening night has arrived, but go on stage and pretend you're still in rehearsal. What can you say to yourself when the scary feelings begin to emerge?

Affirmations

Affirmations are strong statements that "make firm" the positive message you've been practicing. They can be woven into an inner

STEP 6

monologue, spoken out loud, written down, or even sung. Emphasize pairing them with breath and imagery.

- I can cope with these feelings.

- I've been here before and I got through it.

- I've lived through panic before.

- I'm uncomfortable but not dying.

- I'm going to stay here no matter how I feel.

- Slowly my body is learning to relax.

- I'm moving forward.

- This isn't the worst that could happen.

- I can control my fear by controlling my ideas.

- I'll just take my time and practice relaxing.

- I'll just breathe slowly through my belly.

- There's an end to it.

- These feelings are just adrenaline, which will soon wash out of my body.

- I'll keep my mind on right now.

- I've survived this and worse before.

- This too shall pass.

- I'm still standing!

- It's just panic. I'll breathe and wait for it to go away.

- It's already getting better.

STEP 6

Establishing a Memory Bank

Suppose you've successfully lowered anxiety or stopped a panic attack. As we discussed in the previous step, you've just created a powerful memory bank that now has one deposit but will soon be filled with many others. The hard part's finished. From now on, it's just refining your skills and practicing in different situations.

Getting Comfortable with Panic

What if you're still struggling with panic? When you accept "what is," you change. Put another way, when you give up the need to be in control, you take control. Because panic can be scary and uncomfortable, you try hard to prevent it, avoid situations where it might occur, and worry about your ability to cope with it. Let's not forget the self-blame that inevitably develops when you think you've failed at controlling panic, as well as the fear that others will judge you if they know you suffer from panic. When you forgive yourself for having panic attacks, you're accessing a positive emotion, so your heart unclenches and sends a signal to activate the relaxation response.

Naomi Rachel Remen, author of *Kitchen Table Wisdom* (2006), emphasizes that bravery doesn't mean being unafraid; it means being afraid and doing it anyway. Self-judgment, whether in the form of criticism or approval, can stifle our life force because it encourages constant striving. By giving up judgment about having a panic attack and accepting the accompanying sensations, both mind and body relax.

What you believe about yourself can hold you hostage. Remen compares a belief to a pair of sunglasses. When you wear a belief and look at life through those lenses, it's hard to recognize that what you see isn't real. She describes one of the greatest revelations in life as the moment you recognize you're wearing glasses. Remove them and you've released yourself from the shackles of faulty beliefs, attitudes,

STEP 6

judgment, and shame. It's typically the imperfections that draw others closer to us.

The Power of "Yet"

The race isn't won or lost until it's over. Judge something before it's finished and you've jumped to an irrational conclusion. Practice adding the word "yet" and you've found your rational voice. Apply it to a general characteristic, such as "I haven't recognized my courage...yet." Apply it to a specific situation or skill, such as "I haven't felt relaxed after practicing deep breathing...yet."

THINK RATIONALLY AND BRAIN CHEMICALS CHANGE

By directly challenging disturbing thoughts, changing your perceptions, and deleting the judge in your head, you're not only thinking like a scientist, you're altering brain chemicals. Practice putting "so" before the "what if," demand hard proof, and challenge your conclusions by asking, "Where's the evidence?" Think of the worst that could happen and imagine still existing and possibly even enjoying life. Practice rational thinking and slowly, but surely, physiological healing takes place.

Take slow belly breaths, unclench any tight muscles, and create joyful imagery to accompany realistic thinking. See yourself as relaxed and breathe into that vision. Sense warmth flowing through your heart as you awaken love and appreciation and imagine these good feelings being absorbed by every cell. Find a monologue or affirmation that works, perhaps, "So what if I panic? I've been here before and survived," or "It's already getting better." Imagine being a warrior as you feel the strength of each breath and inhale courage. The body knows how to quiet down when the conscious mind steps out

STEP 6

of the way. As you wait patiently for the relaxation response to kick in, tell yourself that you're grateful for the panic experience, as it means your fight or flight response functions well and what's more, you've been presented with a great opportunity to practice newfound skills.

Remember, no single strategy serves as a magic pill. Integrating breathing, muscle release, imagery, and rational thinking changes your brain chemistry enough so that the next time anxiety develops letting go of it will be easier.

PUTTING TOGETHER STEPS 1 THROUGH 6

In Step 6, find your reasoning errors, challenge irrational self-talk by thinking like a scientist, and view panic as an opportunity to practice your new skills.

Here's one example of how to integrate Steps 1 to 6:

Step 1:

+ I won't fear what I'm feeling; it's just panic.

Step 2:

+ My fearful thoughts and negative images about something being wrong set off the alarm system.

Step 3:

+ Slow belly breathing will feel great right now and will gradually cancel the alarm response.

Step 4:

+ My muscles feel tight, so I'll unclench by tightening even more and then letting go.

STEP 6

Step 5:

- I'll imagine becoming more relaxed with each breath cycle.

- I'll shift attention to remembering taking a walk on my favorite beach.

Step 6:

- Where's the evidence that I'm really sick?

- I've been here before and can stand discomfort.

- It's just adrenaline and I'll wait patiently for it to clear my body.

- I'm already getting better.

STEP 6

STEP 7
Distract Yourself

Every technique for stopping a panic attack can be interpreted as a form of distraction. Draw in a slow deep breath, create a positive image, shift to a rational thought, or focus on letting go of muscle tension: they're all diversions from the sensations associated with panic. With Step 7, you'll fully experience the power of distraction, ranging from losing yourself in an outside activity or breaking out in laughter to mindfully turning inward.

MOVING INTO MINDFULNESS

Did you ever catch yourself reading a paragraph, but your mind was somewhere else? Have you noticed this phenomenon in the middle of a conversation when someone else is talking? Have you attempted to focus attention on an external event when you're anxious, but your mind wanted to stay with the panic? Effectively distracting attention away from discomfort involves becoming fully engaged, a process that's often referred to as mindfulness.

Stemming from Buddhist philosophy, mindfulness means getting out of the past or future and completely immersing yourself in the present moment; in other words, being here fully by being completely awake and engaging all the senses. By bringing your attention to one thing, you deepen awareness of the present moment. Dr. Jon Kabat-Zinn refers to mindfulness as the experience of seeing everything as if for the first time. Imagine the feeling of putting on glasses if you're nearsighted, or taking in an experience with a childlike sense of wonder.

By cultivating a beginner's mind, you'll no longer judge in advance how you're going to feel, as no moment is identical to any other. Similarly, by abandoning predetermined agendas and giving up striving for results, you'll accept whatever's occurring in the moment. Mindfulness occurs in real time, so the mind becomes distracted from evaluating the past or future.

Strong research evidence exists linking mindfulness training to the reduction of anxiety and panic. Benefits include a decrease in heart rate and blood pressure. Mindfulness stimulates the left prefrontal cortex, an area of the brain responsible for reduced anxiety and increases in positive emotions. Not only can regular practice decrease anxiety on the spot, physiological changes occur even when you're not practicing mindfulness. Just as runners have a lower heart rate when they're not running, meditators maintain a quieting response throughout the day.

There's no better way to stir up anxiety than to attempt to make the mind go blank or to direct it where it doesn't want to go. Work around this tendency by calling upon your senses: seeing, hearing, smelling, tasting, and touching. By recruiting these pathways, the mind becomes so busy focusing on the external environment that it's not directly attending to anxious thoughts or uncomfortable bodily sensations.

Don't confuse mindfulness with stillness. To prove this point, clap your hands and notice how that action brings you into the present. Practicing mindfulness also doesn't require repeating a mantra or sitting cross-legged on the floor with outstretched arms and palms facing up for an extended period of time. If you have a racing mind, sitting in a meditation class can be torturous. It may be better to ease into mindfulness gradually.

STEP 7

Distract Yourself Visually

Mindfulness implies seeing things as they really are. Start by gazing at any object and studying it with complete awareness. Perhaps look closely at one of the following, as if you were seeing it for the first time:

+ a flower

+ a picture hanging on the wall

+ a tree

+ clouds

+ an object on your desk

+ a burning candle.

What did you notice that you didn't take the time to see before?

Distract Yourself through Listening

Hear the entire range of sounds that surround you to find inner quiet. Notice the soft sounds, the louder ones, the noises, and even the silences. These are some examples:

+ the floorboards creaking

+ whispers in the hallway

+ a clock ticking

+ the hum of air conditioning

+ the honking of a car's horn.

Notice background sounds so deeply that the body "hears" the vibrations deep inside. If thoughts come up, refocus on the sounds. Practice wherever you are. Practice with your eyes open, then shut them and notice the difference.

STEP 7

Listening keeps you in the present moment. These sounds are happening now. Just close your eyes and tune in, as if you're a radio receiver. What can you pick up? Hear the background noises you typically try to tune out. Listen as if you're hearing a symphony.

What soothing sounds do you want to bring into your environment? Most people find that music draws them into a relaxed state.

- Set up a small fountain.

- Create a playlist of nature sounds.

- Create a playlist of music that evokes good feelings.

Distract Yourself through Smell

A pleasant scent can provide a distraction from uncomfortable sensations. Engage your sense of smell with aromatherapy, which involves the use of aromatic oils. (It's important to use 100 percent essential oils without added chemicals.) Keep some in your purse, your car, your desk drawer, and by your bed. Add an essential oil to a damp, warm, or cold washcloth and place it over your eyes, forehead, or feet.

The following are good choices for promoting a relaxation response:

- lavender

- chamomile

- rose

- peppermint

- lemon or lemongrass

- eucalyptus.

STEP 7

When your great-grandmother went for her "smelling salts" during a panic attack to avert fainting, she was engaging in aromatherapy by sniffing ammonia. Fortunately, smelling salts can be made instead with soothing essential oils. Try making your own sachet:

- Mix 1 cup of Epsom salt with ¼ cup of kosher or sea salt.

- Add 6–8 drops of essential oil.

- Place on a piece of cheesecloth and secure tightly or use as a bath salt.

Distract Yourself through Touch

Have you ever walked into a shop where fragile objects are sold and seen a posted sign warning, "Do not touch?" Change that to "Mindfully touch." Fully engage your tactile awareness by noticing every sensation that's involved in the act of touching. Consider these possibilities or invent your own:

- Stroke your pet's fur.

- Feel the warmth of a mug filled with a hot beverage.

- Feel the softness of your "comfy clothes" on your skin.

Distract Yourself through Activity

Mindfully engaging in any type of distracting activity stops panic. Even an action as simple as counting the change in your pocket or purse can work as a distraction. Another simple counting technique entails counting down from 100 to 1, typically saying the number with each exhalation. Counting backwards by 9s is another tool for stopping panic.

Fortunately, everyday life offers many opportunities for practicing mindfulness. Choose a mundane chore where the mind

STEP 7

likes to wander, such as washing the dishes, and turn it into an exercise in experiencing the here and now.

- How fully can you lose yourself in the process of washing dishes?
- Feel the water.
- Smell the soap.
- Watch the water washing over the dish.
- Notice the movement of your arms as you scrub.
- Take it all in as if your senses were newly awakened.

What other repetitive activities present opportunities to practice mindfulness? How about folding the laundry, washing the car, pulling weeds from the garden? One of my personal favorites is cleaning out a drawer or closet.

I once had a client with severe panic attacks that couldn't be controlled despite numerous trials of medication. What worked? Whenever she phoned in the middle of a panic episode, I asked her if there was a closet or drawer that needed to be cleaned out. Sure enough, she called back an hour later reporting that a miracle had occurred: she got so involved in making decisions about what possessions to keep and what to give away that she forgot all about the panic. Soon she moved on to distracting herself through other types of meaningful activity.

What activities bring you joy? Do you have hobbies or special interests that are so engaging you lose yourself in them? Have you ever wanted to pursue such an activity? When you're fully engaged in a pleasurable activity, you're practicing mindfulness.

One of my favorite diversions is knitting, as the soothing, repetitive motion promotes a quieting response. Here's just some of the distractions that knitting provides: listening to the sound of the clicking needles, sensing the movement of your hands, feeling

STEP 7

the texture of the yarn, concentrating on deciphering the written instructions for a particular pattern, looking through books and magazines to find ideas for new projects, and, best of all, taking pride in the finished product. Another positive about knitting is the portability factor, as you can knit just about anywhere.

Any hobby presents opportunities for staying fully focused in the present and may offer a social outlet as well. If it's a new interest, that's even better, as the challenge of learning and practicing something you've never done before requires complete attention. When panic develops, activities that require intense concentration work best. That's why solving a math problem, finishing a puzzle, or playing a card game are better distractions than just turning on the television.

Prepare a Distraction in Advance

In Step 6 we discussed the benefits of rehearsing for situations where panic symptoms are likely to develop. Preparing a diversion can be part of this process. Start by making a list of as many interests or activities that could distract from the panic. What do you want to keep with you? These can all be effective diversions:

- a journal with helpful sayings

- a game

- a deck of cards

- music

- photos

- apps on your smartphone

- a copy of this book.

STEP 7

Distract Yourself through Engagement with Others

If you lose yourself in anxious thoughts or become overwhelmed by panic, you're engaged in a solitary pursuit because you're looking inward. Instead, look outside of yourself and connect with someone else.

- Practice mindfulness by truly listening when someone else is speaking.

- Enhance the distraction potential of a particular activity by sharing the experience with someone else.

- Imagine someone comforting you.

- Is there someone who comforted you in the past? If so, hear their voice soothing you.

Distract Yourself with Laughter

Laughing out loud brings a release of tension. While belly laughing, you exhale more than inhale. If the laugh is big enough, you vigorously exhale by pulling your abdominal muscles to your spine and engaging the diaphragm. More oxygen becomes available for cells and more carbon dioxide is released. Blood pressure, heart rate, and respiration rate all drop, and secretion of cortisol, the stress hormone, decreases. Think of laughter as a much-needed break from stress that gives your body a chance to replenish depleted physical and emotional resources. By laughing, you dissolve distressing emotions, relax and recharge. Deep belly laughter represents the epitome of "letting go." How many times during the day do you break out in laughter? Can you laugh at yourself and abandon self-blame or guilt? Can you take yourself less seriously?

It's impossible to feel angry, sad, tense, or anxious while laughing. Even the anticipation of laughing has stress-reducing benefits. By thinking about something funny, you gain a new perspective for

STEP 7

interpreting situations in a more realistic and less threatening way. As a result, feelings grow more positive.

Consider the ability to laugh; it's the most powerful survival skill that contributes to emotional hardiness. Because it enhances the sense of being in control and instantaneously wipes fear away, humor reduces anxiety more than any other type of distraction. Laughter truly is the best medicine.

There's no such thing as being unable to laugh. An ancient mode of pre-linguistic vocal communication engaged in by babies, laughter remains part of a universal human vocabulary. Unfortunately, as you get older, life becomes more serious, and there may be fewer and fewer opportunities for laughter. But the ability to laugh improves with regular practice. What you lost in the process of growing up can be regained, so that laughing out loud soon becomes a habit. You can even learn to laugh during a panic attack.

Start by practicing laughter yoga, a technique developed by Dr. Gulshan Sethi. Because endorphins are released and the production of stress hormones turns off, laughter yoga can stop a panic response. So start laughing whenever you feel anxious. If you can't produce a genuine belly laugh, fake it. That's laughter yoga.

- Start by imagining yourself laughing.

- Take a breath in by pushing out your belly and then exhale by pulling in your belly. As you exhale, say "ha, ha, ha."

- Say "ha, ha, ha" each time you exhale.

Keep repeating this. If you're thinking you sound stupid, that's good. The sillier you feel, the better. Make faces; stomp around. Force yourself to smile.

- Now add "ho, ho, ho" as you inhale.

You're faking a laugh, but your physical body is getting into a laughter pose.

STEP 7

- Ha, ha, ha, ho, ho, ho!

Is there any humor you can find in this situation?

- Keep going while you remember a time when you couldn't stop laughing.

- Keep repeating while you recall something or someone very funny.

- Imagine being tickled.

- Feel the laughter deep inside you.

Consider deliberate laughter as a form of healthy breathing, which overrides the negative scripts that get stuck in your head. Try accessing the following memories:

- Remember a time when you were convulsing with laughter, a time when you laughed until you cried. Were you anxious, panicked, or worried at that moment?

- Have you ever felt angry or upset and laughing relieved the tension?

- Think of a situation that caused great anxiety. Can you look back and find the humor?

- Imagine you're a stand-up comedian relating the humorous side of a panic attack?

- Can you practice laughing at yourself for starting to panic?

Prepare in advance to use humor as a distraction from panic.

- Make a list of jokes you consider funny.

- Place cartoons in handy locations.

STEP 7

- Go to the American Film Institute's website, get a list of their Top 100 Funniest Movies, and have some ready for viewing.

- Keep your favorite TV comedies readily available.

Distract Yourself through Movement

There's strong and growing evidence suggesting that physical exercise reduces the stress response and significantly improves mood while reducing anxiety and tension. You don't even have to actually exercise to get a small dose of these benefits. Just imagining exercising reduces anxiety.

Exercise fulfills the need to act by fighting or fleeing. In response to intense movement, a message is disseminated that the danger has passed so the alarm system turns off. In addition, sympathetic activation to everyday stressors lessens because physical exertion repeatedly turns on this stress response. Inducing some of the chemical correlates of sympathetic activation improves stress tolerance, as the body gradually adjusts to the physiological consequences of stress.

Physical activity increases the brain's ability to utilize serotonin, dopamine, and norepinephrine, and boosts the production of endorphins, leading to an improved sense of wellbeing. Exercise also releases built-up frustrations, resulting in a more rapid metabolism of excess adrenaline. It reduces skeletal muscle tension and increases body temperature, which leads to a more relaxed state. Because it may involve taking a risk or overcoming a challenge, exercise enhances self-efficacy and positive feelings related to achievement and mastery.

Exercise reduces stress, but only if you're engaging in an activity that you actually want to do. How does it feel when you're forced into something? Have you ever started an exercise program or joined a gym with the best of intentions, only to drop out or discontinue? Are

STEP 7

you having fun or is it drudgery? Negative thinking about having to exercise cancels out the anxiety-reducing benefits.

If you're resistant to exercise, ask yourself, "Why?" Start by taking a look at your beliefs or excuses about not exercising. Do any of the following sound familiar?

- I don't have time.

- I'm too tired.

- It's boring.

- It's inconvenient.

- I'm too old.

- I'm too overweight and out of shape.

- I haven't found any activity I like.

- I hated gym in school.

- I tried exercise and it didn't work.

- I'll get too anxious and have a panic attack.

- I'm afraid of exercise.

My own early memories of physical activity were anything but positive. Upon leaving my first aerobics class, I felt my heart pounding, my legs shaking and, fearing I was about to faint, considered going straight to the emergency room.

What didn't I know then that I know now? For one thing, strenuous physical exercise causes blood levels of sodium lactate to rise, which may have triggered the onset of a panic attack because I didn't recognize why these sensations were occurring. I probably misinterpreted other signs of aerobic exertion, such as rapid heartbeat, feeling warm, or sweating, as indicative of physical illness. Reacting to the new experience of exercising by scaring myself, I

STEP 7

could have easily reached the irrational conclusion that exercise wasn't for me. Now I look forward to daily exercise as a source of mental joy and physical bliss.

Want to distract yourself from negative thoughts? Get up and move. Can you find joy in movement? Any form of movement that you enjoy creates a relaxation response.

Take a Walk

Walking can be a powerful moving meditation. If you typically fill your mind with chatter and anxiety-producing thoughts when attempting to sit quietly, take a walk instead.

- As you walk, inhale wonderful sensations and savor long exhalations.

- Open your senses to whatever attracts your attention.

- Observe the flow of images, sounds, smells, and feelings.

Do Some Yoga Poses

A moving meditation that connects mind and body and links breath to movement, yoga represents the epitome of mindfulness and regular practice helps to minimize anxiety. Think of yoga as preventative and positive medicine that decreases cortisol, the stress hormone, and turns on a relaxation response by activating the parasympathetic branch of the autonomic nervous system.

Yoga may alter brain chemistry more directly and efficiently than regular exercise, as it provides the brain with a balance of stimulation and relaxation. Increases in alpha wave activity, the brain wave state associated with relaxation, and theta brain waves, associated with daydreaming and reverie, have been directly tied to yoga. Other physiological changes include elevations of GABA, an inhibitory neurotransmitter that induces a calm state, and increases in heart

STEP 7

rate variability, also linked with inner quiet. Furthermore, yoga has been found to promote increased delivery of oxygen and glucose to the brain.

Because the most significant feature of yoga lies in the use of breath, you're already doing yoga if you're practicing slow abdominal breathing. Yoga can be practiced anytime, anyplace, or anywhere. The only requirement: inhaling and exhaling breath.

Far from being uniform, styles of yoga differ considerably, ranging from restorative, gentle, yin yoga to strength-building power yoga. Classes can be found at the local health club or at dedicated studios. Sometimes the room may be heated for a detoxifying "hot yoga" experience. But although the physical surroundings, choice of specific poses, transitions between poses, length of time holding each pose, and total time devoted to the practice vary considerably, the ingredients that make yoga so beneficial hold constant.

If you attended a class or tried practicing at home and the experience turned out to be unpleasant or anxiety-provoking, figure out what went wrong. Was the class too advanced, too easy, too crowded, or too warm? Did the teacher give unclear directions or fail to provide enough individualized attention? Did you attempt to practice from a book or DVD as a first experience and need more guidance?

First and foremost, find a well-trained teacher who teaches a class that offers options to accommodate all levels. For example, the use of blocks can make up for lack of mobility and prevent injury. If a particular class or style of yoga isn't working for you, find another one that may be more suitable. Finding the right program can be intimidating or confusing. To prevent negative consequences, choose a style that's right for you. If you associate panic attacks with feeling warm, avoid hot yoga. If your mind wanders, you may prefer an active vinyasa flow class to yin, or restorative, yoga. To attain the most anxiety-reducing benefit, give your critical mind a rest when you step onto your mat. Avoid letting effort and self-evaluation get in the way. Judith Lasater, author of *Relax and Renew* (2011), refers

STEP 7

to yoga as a practice of happiness and suggests saying, "How human of me" while moving through various poses. So what if you can't do what the person on the next mat is doing with ease.

After you've taken some classes and feel comfortable with basic poses, you're ready to use yoga to prevent or stop a panic attack. A few favorite postures can provide everything you need. No matter which poses you choose, they all offer opportunities to practice mindfulness and distract you from anxious feelings. Just move with your breath and pay conscious attention to good physical sensations, thoughts, and emotions.

Practice yoga to maintain a calm state and prevent the onset of panic by weaving yoga poses into your daily life. While attending a class offers the most benefits, any amount of time yields positive results. Set an intention to practice for 20 minutes every morning and evening. If that's not working, commit to 10 minutes. Look for opportunities to strike a yoga pose whenever the spirit moves you. We're going to explore the anxiety-reducing power of forward bends and legs up the wall.

Do Some Forward Bends

Forward bends calm the nervous system. Child's Pose is a great anxiety-reducing forward bend that anyone can practice (although avoid during pregnancy or if you have knee or ankle injuries).

- Get on your hands and knees.

- Point your toes on the floor and separate your knees about hip-width apart.

- Slowly lower your buttocks towards your heels. Place a pillow, towel or yoga block under your buttocks if the stretch across the knees feels uncomfortable.

STEP 7

- Relax your chin and let your forehead rest on the floor. Place your forehead on a pillow if your head doesn't easily rest on the floor.

- Place your arms at your sides, palms up, or outstretched in front of you.

- Breathe slowly with your belly.

Child's Pose I

Child's Pose II

STEP 7

Put Your Legs up the Wall

Choose legs up the wall if you want to find complete physical stillness. I frequently teach it to clients who are looking for a quick way to quiet the nervous system and ease muscle fatigue. What's more, it offers a perfect opportunity to practice slow belly breathing. This restorative pose feels great at the end of the day, and I often rely on it to distract myself from stressful events, find inner quiet, and prepare for a good night's rest. Try these suggestions for putting your legs up the wall:

- Find some space in front of a wall.

- Turn on some soothing music.

- If desired, place a blanket (folded lengthwise), bolster, or pillow under your lower back to boost the restorative power of this pose. Place it with the long edge running parallel to the wall, leaving a gap of just a few inches between the support and the wall.

- Sit with the left side of your body parallel to the wall and as close to it as you can get.

- Using your hands for support, shift your weight onto the outer right hip. Next lower your right shoulder to the floor so that you can pivot your pelvis and raise your legs up the wall.

- Settle your back onto the floor so that you're perpendicular to the wall. If you're too far from the wall, get on your elbows and shimmy closer.

- Let your shoulder blades rest comfortably on the floor.

- Feel your heels touching the wall and allow your feet to turn away from one another.

STEP 7

- Ideally, keep your legs straight.

- If moving close to the wall feels uncomfortable, bend your legs and slide the support a few inches away from the wall. Experiment with the distance between the support and the wall until you find a comfortable position that gently stretches the backs of your legs.

- Try placing a rolled up towel under your neck.

- Rest your arms in a comfortable position, either out to the sides, palms unclenched and facing up, or on your belly.

- Close your eyes. Perhaps place an eye bag over your eyes, particularly one that's scented with lavender.

- Observe your slow belly breathing as you surrender into the surface beneath you.

- Scan your body and imagine the tension dissolving completely.

- Imagine the feeling of tranquility.

- Let the cares of the day drain from your legs.

- Imagine every last drop of tension melting away.

- Invite tranquility to fill every ounce of your being.

- Stay in the pose for as long as you like.

- When you feel deliciously relaxed, slowly slide your legs down the wall, bending your knees close to your chest. Rest here for a few moments before rolling onto your right side and using your hand to very slowly sit up.

STEP 7

Legs up the wall

Even if you're in a situation where physically assuming a yoga position is out of the question, use your imagination and pretend you're doing yoga. Remember, what's "Real in the mind is real in the body." Even if you're not actively practicing, commit to an inner practice throughout the day to shed anxiety and become more at ease.

Distract Yourself with Tai Chi or Qi Gong

I chose to emphasize the benefits of yoga but two other time-honored movement traditions yield similar results: tai chi and qi gong. They're both moving meditations and are extremely gentle to the body. Consider these ancient practices as wonderful alternatives if you have a negative reaction to yoga.

Tai chi, a form of movement that unites mind and body, is believed to restore the flow of *chi*, or energy, and create a state of balance. Qi gong, pronounced "chee-gong," dates back at least two

STEP 7

thousand years. Similar to tai chi, by integrating meditation, breathing and movement, the practice helps to resolve energy blockages, so that *chi* can flow freely.

Distract Yourself by Becoming More Mindful of Anxiety

Panic itself can become the object of focused attention. Let go of the need to do anything about anxious feelings or uncomfortable physical sensations; just stay fully aware of them without judgment or self-condemnation. What would happen if you observed, and paid close attention to, the panic from moment to moment? You won't die from experiencing uncomfortable sensations. By uncritically accepting whatever you're experiencing, the judging mind backs off and the demand to get somewhere else ceases. What's the result? The relaxation response kicks in. It's even possible to laugh at panic, a surefire way to eliminate it.

Paying close attention to everything you're feeling will result in noticing bits of comfort beneath the anxiety, as panic varies in intensity from one moment to the next. You may also discover that panic, like everything else, is transitory, a temporary negative state similar to boredom or sadness.

PUTTING TOGETHER STEPS 1 THROUGH 7

Use the following example to practice what you've learned so far, but substitute or add your own variations to personalize your practice:

Step 1:

- It's just panic and you've been here before, so let go of "fearing fear."

STEP 7

Step 2:

- You're not physically or mentally ill.

- You've set off your alarm system with scary thoughts and now it's working exquisitely well to protect you from perceived danger.

Step 3:

- Start taking slow belly breaths to shut off the alarm system.

Step 4:

- Unclench your muscles, as they don't need to tighten up in preparation to fight or run away.

Step 5:

- Imagine a wonderful place where you can feel something good.

- Imagine good feelings developing right now.

Step 6:

- Repeat to yourself: "So what if I've worked myself up to a panic attack? The feelings are uncomfortable but not awful, horrible or terrible."

- "I can tolerate the panic and I'll soon feel better."

Step 7:

- While waiting for the panic to pass, find an engaging distraction.

- Take a walk and notice every detail you see, hear, smell, or touch.

STEP 7

STEP 8
Eat Calming Foods

In Steps 1 through 7 we looked at the benefits of replacing negative thoughts, images, and breathing patterns with more soothing ones and adding physical movement and positive connections to quiet both your mind and your body. Now let's dig deeper and discuss causes of panic that you might be overlooking. What irritating foods may be contributing to panic and anxiety? What toxic chemicals assault the body? What nutrients may be lacking? Would supplementation with vitamins, minerals, or herbs be helpful?

Food isn't just calories. The right amount of the right foods can be more powerful than any medicine, while the wrong amount of the wrong foods leads to harmful consequences. A key principle of functional medicine involves taking out what's bad for you. You may not realize that the foods you're eating could be contributing to your anxiety.

There's considerable research to support the relationship between food and mood, but when you think of anxiety, you may not be associating it with nutritional needs. Yet poor food choices and eating habits can create constant stress. Some foods promote a calm, quiet state while others promote anxiety. We're only just beginning to explore the effect of environmental toxins on brain health.

The foods you consume might be overly refined and processed, and filled with chemicals and hormones. These "food-like" substances, so different from the fresh foods that your great-grandparents ate, tax your gastrointestinal tract and detoxification systems, signal the overproduction of insulin, and stress the adrenal glands. What if removing these irritants from your diet proved to be one of the most significant steps towards stopping panic?

REMOVE THE BAD STUFF
Eliminate Sugar

More addictive than alcohol, cocaine, or heroin, sugar places an enormous stress on the body, not only triggering a surge of the stress hormones cortisol and adrenaline, but also leading to inflammation due to the overproduction of insulin. After eating something sweet, blood sugar levels may shoot up too quickly, resulting in a corresponding rush of insulin production. When insulin levels rise, blood sugar levels drop too low, resulting in wide swings in blood sugar and, ultimately, overall low blood sugar, referred to as hypoglycemia. Blood sugar disregulation may result in feeling "high" after consuming sugar, but spacey 20–30 minutes afterwards.

Dizziness, disorientation, mental fog, fatigue, trembling, heart palpitations, weakness, or irritability have been associated with low blood sugar levels. If you awaken in a state of panic, you may do so because blood sugar levels are generally lowest in the early morning due to having fasted all night. If blood sugar levels are too high, such as immediately after eating a big piece of cake, you might feel revved up, agitated, or overly stimulated. I'm all too familiar with this syndrome and, in hindsight, recognize it as a major contributor to my panic attacks.

Not all carbohydrates affect blood sugar and insulin production in the same way. If you eat fruits and vegetables, these carbohydrates have lots of fiber, a tough substance which takes a long time to be broken down by the digestive enzymes and converted into glucose for fuel. Consequently, you won't experience a sugar rush. By providing a slow, steady release of glucose into the system, including the brain, carbohydrates in fruits and vegetables offer a stable way to feel alert, balanced, and energized. Given my "sweet tooth" and

STEP 8

resulting problems with insulin dysregulation, I feel best when sticking with carbohydrates in the form of vegetables, and limit my fruit consumption to low-sugar choices such as berries.

Processed foods containing sugar or flour, such as cookies, crackers, breads, and most cereals, are already broken down, which means the body doesn't have to work very hard to convert them to blood sugar. As a result, they send blood sugar levels skyrocketing, followed by the inevitable crash that leaves you craving another fix to raise your blood sugar. The sudden influx of glucose triggers an equally sudden surge of insulin. Concentrated fruit juices and soft drinks may be the worst offenders, as they jolt the system with a "shot of sugar."

A high glycemic diet favors glutamate production. Glutamate is the primary excitatory neurotransmitter in the brain and it opposes the action of GABA, the inhibitory neurotransmitter associated with a quieting response. Glutamate is produced from circulating glucose. All glucose that makes its way to the brain converts to glutamate at one point or another. High glucose loads create the potential for the over production of glutamate, especially in the presence of low vitamin B6 or high levels of the artificial sweetener, aspartame.

Overconsumption of sugar, amongst other factors, may also lead to an overgrowth of the yeast variety, candida albicans. Symptoms associated with this condition include feelings of unreality, brain fog, and chest tightness, all of which mimic panic sensations. If you have sugar cravings and experience these symptoms, I recommend a nutritional consultation regarding a specialized diet for candida.

Are you ready to eliminate sugar and want more support? My colleague, Dr. Mark Hyman, chairman of the Institute for Functional Medicine, offers a detailed guide to kicking the sugar habit in his best-selling book *The 10-Day Detox Diet* (2014).

STEP 8

Eliminate Artificial Sweeteners

Artificial sweeteners can cause anxiety or make existing anxiety worse. Aspartame, for example, may increase the symptoms of anxiety because it stimulates certain receptors in the brain (N-methyl-D-aspartate, or NMDA), to overproduce glutamate, resulting in neuroexcitatory effects. Fake sweeteners also "light up the pleasure center" in your brain, causing you to continue to crave the taste of something sweet. How many artificially sweetened products are you consuming every day? Do you drink diet sodas, chew sugarless gum, or add these toxic substances to your coffee?

Eliminate Caffeine

When you consume caffeine, the sympathetic branch of the autonomic nervous system turns on and releases adrenaline. Norepinephrine levels elevate and, as a result, you feel wide awake. This may be okay for some, but if you're prone to panic you may overreact to substances which affect the central nervous system. Drinking even one cup of coffee may trigger a panic attack. What's more, that cup of coffee you drank in the morning to wake up may stay in your system for longer than you realize and can contribute to feeling anxious throughout the day and even into the evening. As an alternative, consider switching to green tea. Although caffeinated, this beneficial tea also contains l-theanine, a nutrient that promotes a relaxation response and blocks the absorption of caffeine.

Reduce Alcohol Intake

Withdrawal from alcohol causes anxiety, which is most likely due to imbalances in the neurotransmitter system, particularly involving GABA. While ingestion of alcohol causes an over-facilitation of GABA in the brain, when you stop drinking, GABA levels drop, increasing the likelihood of anxiety.

STEP 8

Determine If You Have Food Sensitivities or Intolerances

Allergies are easy to detect: you eat something and immediately develop a rash or hives. Food sensitivities may not be as obvious, but could be causing symptoms such as heart palpitations, dizziness, or other sensations associated with panic. Although food sensitivities may be pervasive in modern societies, they're hard to recognize. You could be reacting to certain foods and not know it.

You might be sensitive to the foods you crave the most and these cravings may have led to a state of imbalance. Gluten (a protein found primarily in wheat, barley, and rye), dairy, corn, and soy are common offenders. Your immune cells could be reacting to these foods as foreign invaders and activating the stress response, leading to inflammation.

In addition to food sensitivities, consider the presence of food intolerances (which differ from food allergies and sensitivities as an immune response isn't involved). For example, some people have adverse reactions to the lactose found in milk. You may be familiar with histamine and the immediate inflammatory response it causes if you suffer from seasonal allergies. If you have an intolerance of histamine-rich foods (fermented foods, vinegar, cured meats, aged cheeses, and many others) you could experience anxiety as one of the symptoms. Another possible source of food intolerance is salicylates, the chemicals found in many plants that act as a natural pesticide. They're found in a variety of medications, fruits, vegetables, herbs, spices, teas, food additives, and fragrances. Salicylate intolerance has been associated with rapid heart rate, anxiety and panic attacks.

How do you know if you have hidden food sensitivities or intolerances? Although blood tests are available that measure the number of antibodies produced in reaction to a wide range of foods, the most accurate and economical way to find out which foods you may be sensitive to or intolerant of, involves going on an elimination diet. Keep in mind that if you have food intolerances, testing for antibodies won't be helpful, as intolerances aren't immune reactions.

STEP 8

There are several ways to embark on an elimination diet. One option would be to take out one potential irritant at a time for three to four weeks. Which of the following would you start with?

- sugar

- gluten

- dairy

- soy

- corn.

Is there another food group that you suspect might be the culprit?

A second option would be to refrain from eating gluten, dairy, and sugar for three to four weeks, as these are the most problematic foods for optimal brain health. A comprehensive elimination diet involves avoiding all of the above, plus corn, soy, eggs, peanuts, red meat, caffeine, and foods containing nitrates. During this time, consider eliminating all processed foods.

After the three to four-week period ends, food groups can be added by to your diet one at a time. However, chances are you'll feel so good that you'll want to permanently avoid some of these irritants, particularly sugar and gluten. Many of my clients notice considerable reduction in anxiety after following this plan.

The comprehensive elimination diet has proven to be one of the most powerful tools in the functional medicine practitioner's tool kit. We generally begin with eliminating common food sensitivities and, if this approach doesn't yield good results, dig deeper and look at eliminating sources of specific food intolerances, such as histamine or salicylate-rich foods. I encourage you to find a functional medicine-trained healthcare professional who can personalize an elimination diet for you. Refer to the Institute for Functional Medicine website (www.functionalmedicine.org) for a list of practitioners.

STEP 8

Reduce Toxic Load

Consider for a moment the sheer volume of chemicals that you're exposed to on a daily basis. You're probably eating food laden with additives, artificial colors, artificial flavors, and pesticides. You're likely exposed to toxic environmental pollutants in your home, your workplace, and when you step outside. Personal care products and toiletries, such as shampoos, deodorants, lotions, moisturizers, aftershave, cosmetics, perfumes, and hand sanitizers all contain chemicals and dyes. Add household cleaning products, insecticides, plastics, and heavy metals, such as mercury, lead, arsenic, and cadmium, which lurk in sources ranging from food to dental work. Now throw into the mix the increasing number of electronic devices such as microwave ovens, wireless routers, smart meters, cordless telephones, and cellular phones that create electromagnetic fields.

These hundreds of chemical substances are potentially toxic to the brain. Exposure adds to your overall stress level by overtaxing the adrenal glands, and may either directly or indirectly contribute to a panic reaction. Symptoms associated with sensitivity to chemicals include "brain fog," irritability, and insomnia.

My intake evaluation includes questions about toxic burden. If you were my client, I would want to know if you have a mouthful of silver, mercury-containing fillings, eat a lot of fish high in mercury, recently remodeled your home, work around chemicals, drink from plastic water bottles, use hand sanitizer containing triclosan, or use personal care products containing chemicals such as parabens and sodium laurel sulfates. I would inquire about a host of other subtle chemical exposures, as well as physical symptoms indicative of potential toxic overload, including constipation, rarely sweating (one of the ways the body removes toxins), and sensitivities to odors, such as perfumes.

The brain is exquisitely sensitive to the damaging effects of high toxic burden. For example, I've seen a number of children diagnosed with panic disorder who had also been diagnosed with sensory-integration problems. My hunch was that they were reacting to environmental chemicals, as they often complained about sensitivity to clothing fibers or certain odors. Panic symptoms lessened when exposure levels decreased and specific foods and nutrients were added to boost their ability to detoxify.

It's wise to eliminate as many toxins as possible, including those from food, cleaning products, and personal care items. The Environmental Working Group (www.ewg.org) is a wonderful resource where more information can be obtained about this topic. I also recommend seeking the advice of a healthcare professional trained in functional medicine to determine your degree of toxic burden and help you embark on a personalized metabolic detoxification program. These physicians can also determine if you have a common genetic variation that makes it more difficult for your body to rid itself of toxins.

REPAIR THE BODY

Heal the Gut

We have a second brain: it's called the gut. This brain possesses its own nervous system, the enteric nervous system, which contains more neurons than the spinal cord. The majority of serotonin is produced by these nerve cells and most of the fibers in the vagus nerve carry information from the gut to the brain. The brain experiences everything that happens in the gut, either directly, via the central nervous system, or indirectly due to immune activity. When you get "butterflies" in your stomach or have a strong "gut reaction," that's the gut–brain connection at work.

One of the Institute for Functional Medicine's mantras, "heal the gut," implies that in order for the brain to be in balance, the gut must be in balance. Gastrointestinal conditions such as irritable bowel syndrome (IBS) have been linked to anxiety, based on the assumption that an anxious mind leads to gastrointestinal disturbances. Now there's evidence that anxiety may originate in the gut.

STEP 8

The beneficial bacteria residing in the gut perform many critical functions, including influencing brain chemistry. If the normal bacterial content of the gut is disrupted for any reason, such as antibiotic use, an increase in brain-derived neurotrophic factor (BDNF) occurs. BDNF has been linked to anxiety as well as depression. Recent research demonstrates the benefit of supplementation with probiotics (various strains of friendly bacteria) for the treatment of anxiety disorders, particularly those associated with gastrointestinal conditions.

Some excellent resources for learning how to use a functional medicinal approach to healing the gut are *Digestive Wellness* (2012) by Liz Lipski, and *The Inside Tract* (2011) by Dr. Gerald Mullin and Kathie Madonna Swift.

Put Out the Fire of Inflammation

Eating a "junk food" diet of highly processed foods, the presence of food sensitivities, and environmental stressors all contribute to an inflammatory response within the body. The brain isn't insulated from inflammation. Anxiety, depression, and a host of other conditions previously thought to be "all in the mind" might be the end result of having a brain that's "on fire." What can you do to "put out the fire"? Stop eating inflammatory substances, such as sugar, gluten, and dairy, and eat anti-inflammatory foods instead. You'll get a list of the healing foods that come from nature's "farmacy" later in this step.

Balance Your Hormones

Maybe you're experiencing heart palpitations, dizziness or dry mouth, all familiar signs of panic disorder. But how many of the following symptoms also sound familiar?

- tired upon waking

STEP 8

- difficulty falling asleep and/or staying asleep

- feeling both wired and exhausted

- falling asleep in the afternoon or dozing while reading

- generalized weakness

- weight gain around the midline

- loss of muscle mass

- frequent headaches

- swollen ankles

- hypoglycemia

- needing caffeine or sugary snacks to get through the day

- irritability

- listlessness

- low sex drive

- trouble concentrating.

If you have panic attacks, you may characterize yourself as "wired." But are you both "tired and wired" at the same time? If so, you may have reached a state of adrenal exhaustion, which develops when these glands cannot adequately meet the demands of chronic stress and toxic burden.

Excessive production of cortisol leads to imbalances in the production of other hormones, including insulin, thyroid, and the sex hormones, estrogen and testosterone. High cortisol levels contribute to digestive problems, depression, difficulty concentrating, memory problems, and, last, but not least, anxiety. Eventually, adrenal fatigue sets in as the output of cortisol diminishes due to overstimulation. How do you balance your hormones in order to prevent or reverse

STEP 8

this process? Every time you practice one of the 10 steps outlined in this book, you're balancing your hormones.

Boost Energy Metabolism and Enhance Detoxification
Panic attacks might be a signal that something is out of balance. Besides paying attention to the role of the gut, the presence of inflammation and hormonal imbalances, two other key components for health need to be considered: energy metabolism at a cellular level and detoxification pathways. Are your mitochondria, the "batteries" in your cells that create energy, able to produce enough for you to feel alert and think clearly? Besides being extremely dependent on sufficient nutrients, energy metabolism can also be interrupted if you have a heavy toxic load. That leads to the next question. Are you giving your body the right nutrients to properly eliminate environmental toxins and internal metabolic waste products?

To create balance in the mind, these core processes must function well. How do you create this optimal state? Think food first. You restore the body by feeding it the raw materials essential for life: whole, real foods rich in nutrients in combination with the other ingredients we've covered so far, such as relaxed breathing, positive images, rational thoughts, exercise that's fun, laughter, and social connections.

PUT IN THE GOOD STUFF

A well-fed brain equals a healthy brain. Building brain cells and keeping the communications systems running efficiently requires the raw materials that come from food. There's even a field of study called nutrigenomics that addresses how food affects genes. Various foods contain information that either turn on the expression of particular genes or turn it off.

STEP 8

Everything we eat affects stress levels and emotional states. Both the macronutrients (proteins, fats, and carbohydrates) and micronutrients (vitamins, minerals, and phytonutrients, the colorful pigments in plant foods) act as powerful neurochemicals. A deficiency in even one of these nutrients creates imbalance and compromises brain health. As a result, your response to stress deteriorates and you react with anxiety. Furthermore, if you're facing chronic stress or carry around a high amount of environmental toxins, the need for a balanced blend of nutrients increases.

It's possible to become more aware of the changes that occur after consuming particular foods. Some foods may have a cooling effect while others induce a warming response. Consume mostly raw vegetables, fruits, and salads one day and then eat cooked stews, thick soups, or casseroles the following day. Raw foods might make you feel lighter and more energized, while cooked foods lead to feeling satisfied, content, and warm.

Pay attention to everything you eat and notice how various foods make you feel. Notice any differences in mental clarity or energy level. Which ones result in feeling calm and contented? Observe how removing the bad stuff and adding nourishing foods leads to increased resiliency and less anxiety. You may notice the difference immediately after eating, but often the positive effects of significant dietary changes don't become apparent until a few months down the road.

One of my clients noticed a significant diminishment in her anxiety levels after eliminating gluten, sugar, and dairy. She reported no panic attacks for about four months, but then one day she was out with friends and decided to have some pizza. What was the result? That evening she experienced significant gastrointestinal distress and the next day had a full-blown panic attack. This isn't a rare occurrence, I've seen anxiety reactions that were under control triggered anew by reactions to inflammatory foods such as sugar, gluten, and dairy.

The most important decision you make each day is what you choose to place on the end of your fork, words of advice I learned

STEP 8

from functional medicine expert, Dr. Mark Hyman. But what constitutes a healthy diet to promote brain health? Feeding your mind the right nutrients means eating real foods. Michael Pollan, author of *Food Rules* (2010), recommends avoiding anything your great-grandmother wouldn't recognize as food. The top three anti-anxiety "medicines" to add to your diet are vegetables (particularly dark leafy greens), good quality protein, and healthy fats, including nuts and seeds. Also add some fermented foods to maintain gut health.

Eat Your Vegetables

It seems our mothers were right after all when they admonished us to eat our vegetables. A plant-based diet boosts the production of glutathione, an antioxidant critical for brain health and energy production, which also protects against oxidation (meaning your cells are essentially rusting), controls inflammation, and helps with elimination of toxins.

Specific nutrients in plants, called phytonutrients, activate the Nrf2 pathway (nuclear factor-like2), an important antioxidant response factor, which in turn generates glutathione production at the cellular level to prevent oxidative stress. Vegetables contain a life force or living energy that can have an almost immediate effect on energy level and mood.

If you want to feel calmer, eat more vegetables. Due to their light, watery quality, vegetables help energy move freely throughout the body, resulting in a peaceful feeling. However, frying, grilling, roasting, or baking these foods may not have the same beneficial effects as eating them raw, steamed, stewed, fermented, or in a soup.

You can protect your brain and enhance its functioning by eating a variety of vegetables, especially greens. Choose organic whenever possible to reduce toxic burden from pesticides. Aim for about 10–13 servings each day, with a serving being roughly a cup of greens and half a cup of starchy vegetables. How many of the following, which is by no means an exhaustive list, can you incorporate into your diet?

STEP 8

GREEN, GLORIOUS GREEN

- kale
- collard greens
- Swiss chard
- bok choy
- parsley
- arugula
- dandelion greens

- mustard greens
- romaine and other lettuces
- broccoli
- cabbage
- asparagus
- watercress
- spinach

Fill your plate with greens first, and then add other vegetables to obtain "little bits of a lot of color" in order to get a variety of phytochemicals. Go for rich, vibrant colors, as these pigments are actually important phytonutrients. These phytochemicals, called flavonoids, play a key role in helping your body eliminate toxic load. When you consume a rainbow of colors each day, rather than storing toxins and allowing them to interfere with metabolic processes and affect your brain health, these phytonutrients get to work on detoxification of the "bad stuff" that you don't want to hold on to.

How can you add more color to your diet? Remember that green is the most important color, so go for greens first. As if you were painting a picture, cover your canvas with shades of green, then add specks of vibrant colors. Don't forget to add some white or beige as well.

Although we're stressing the importance of vegetables, fruits are also loaded with phytochemicals, particularly berries. Keep in mind that eating too many fruits might lead to increased anxiety because many varieties are high in sugar. Many of my clients, particularly women, grab a banana as their breakfast while rushing out of the house in the morning. That was how I started the day for many years. What I didn't realize back then was that a banana is high in sugar. Mistakenly believing that I had cured my sugar addiction and was

STEP 8

eating in a healthy way, this was not the case. By eating only a banana, or sometimes combining it with an apple, store-bought yogurt, or some cereal (foods that also turn to sugar), I was getting no protein or fat to feed my brain, and was essentially eating dessert for breakfast. No wonder I often felt light-headed, fatigued, or nervous during the day. Now I know better and either eat some eggs with avocado or make a green smoothie loaded with protein and fats. I limit my intake of fruit primarily to berries, and aim for no more than half a cup a day.

In addition to eating fruits in moderation, beware of the sugar in starchy vegetables. Keep in mind that plants store sugar in their roots, so limit your intake of root vegetables, such as carrots, sweet potatoes, white potatoes, parsnips, and squashes, to no more than one serving a day (about half a cup).

EAT THE RAINBOW
Reds:

- strawberries
- raspberries
- tomatoes
- cherries
- red grapes
- red peppers

- apples
- pomegranate
- cranberries
- radishes
- plums

Oranges:

- carrots
- apricots
- orange bell pepper
- cantaloupe
- mango

- orange
- sweet potato
- turmeric root
- butternut squash
- acorn squash

STEP 8

Blues/Purples:

- blueberries
- blackberries
- eggplant (aubergine)
- purple cabbage

- purple grapes
- purple plums
- figs
- prunes

Whites/Tans/Yellows:

- onions
- garlic
- shallots
- leeks
- sesame seeds
- tahini

- hummus
- ginger
- cinnamon
- nuts
- yellow peppers

EXPERIMENT WITH SEA VEGETABLES

When choosing which vegetables to eat, I bet you're not considering sea vegetables. These nutritional gems are packed with minerals, aid in detoxification, are powerful antioxidants, and help prevent oxidative stress.

- kelp
- nori
- wakame
- hijicki

- dulse
- laver
- arame

STEP 8

Eat Good Quality Proteins

Without an adequate amount of protein at each meal, the brain can't function properly. Proteins contain amino acids, the raw materials needed to make neurotransmitters. Without a steady supply of amino acids, the body has no way to manufacture these neurotransmitters.

If you're eating a breakfast loaded with sugar and refined flours, such as a bowl of dry cereal or a sweet roll, or having just a banana or an apple like I used to do, switch to a protein-based breakfast and notice how different you feel. You'll have more energy, increased alertness, and feel calmer. If you start the day with a protein meal, you'll be getting all the amino acids needed to produce the neurotransmitters that are so essential for optimal brain functioning. If you eat a small protein snack mid-morning and afternoon, you'll also be feeding your mind some wellness.

Just what constitutes good quality protein? If you eat animal protein, think about "what *what you eat* eats." Look for 100 percent grass-fed rather than grain-fed meat, as the latter have been linked to inflammation. Avoid eating animals or animal by-products that have been given antibiotics or hormones. Look to any of the following foods to meet your protein needs:

- sardines, mackerel, anchovies, wild salmon, herring (SMASH)*

- 100 per cent grass-fed beef, lamb, or bison

- pasture-raised chicken

- pasture-raised pork

- organic turkey

- pasture-raised eggs

---

* These fish are preferred over other varieties because they're high in omega 3 fats and low in mercury.

* organic legumes (beans such as lentils, chickpeas, black beans, navy beans)

* non-genetically modified soy, preferably fermented products such as miso and tempeh.

Keep in mind that if you suffer from anxiety or panic attacks you may also have digestive issues as well. If this is the case, then consider eliminating all beans from your diet, including soy. It wasn't until I gave up eating legumes (as well as all types of grains) that I finally felt my body was in balance. If you want to learn more about why legumes and grains might be problematic, I suggest reading *The Wahl's Protocol* (2014) by Dr. Terry Wahls. Although it's a guide to overcoming multiple sclerosis, it's written from a functional medicine perspective and the recommendations can be applied to any condition, including anxiety.

Consume Healthy Fats

Do you need an oil change? Compared to our ancestors, we're eating more refined omega 6 oils, such as corn, soy, sunflower, and safflower oils, and less omega 3 fats, which come primarily from wild-caught fish.

The brain is mostly fat, and omega 3 fatty acids, composed of DHA (docosahexaenoic acid) and EPA (eicosapentaenoic acid), are the most important ingredients for brain health. Not only a critical building block for the membranes that surround brain cells, DHA also plays a role in the transmission of information from one neuron to the next, the control of inflammation and the modulation of gene expression for the production of BDNF. EPA tames inflammation and low levels have been associated with anxiety and depression. Monounsaturated omega 9s, such as avocado and olive oil, are also powerful anti-inflammatory agents.

Saturated fat from animal products and plant sources such as coconut earned a bad reputation and many of us avoided it to

STEP 8

prevent high cholesterol and heart disease. The hypothesis that eating too much saturated fat harms your cardiovascular system has been questioned and many experts now believe that it's fine to include dietary sources of cholesterol in your diet. Your brain needs cholesterol and your hormones are produced from cholesterol. What are good sources of fat?

- SMASH fish (sardines, mackerel, anchovies, wild salmon, herring) for their omega 3 fats

- avocados

- extra virgin olive oil

- unrefined coconut oil

- ghee (clarified butter)

- butter from pasture-raised cows

- tallow, lard

- raw nuts and seeds (consumed whole or made into butters, not processed into oils).

For more information on increasing fat consumption for brain health, while simultaneously lowering sugar and gluten consumption, refer to *Grain Brain* (2013) by Dr. David Perlmutter, a world-renowned functional medicine expert.

Eat Fermented Foods

Fermented, or cultured foods, such as yogurt, sauerkraut, kimchi (spicy fermented cabbage popular in Korea) and miso (fermented soybean paste), contain probiotic bacteria. As mentioned earlier, the microorganisms that live in our gut play a key role in digestion and have a positive effect on brain functioning. These beneficial bacteria

STEP 8

may affect GABA, the inhibitory neurotransmitter that reduces the activity of neurons and contributes to the release of less cortisol.

Discover Raw Nuts and Seeds

Raw nuts and seeds make great snacks. Enjoy all varieties, including almonds, walnuts, pecans, cashews, hazelnuts, macadamia nuts, and Brazil nuts. Rather than sticking with peanut butter (actually a legume and high in a mold called alflatoxin), try other nut butters such as almond butter or cashew butter. Seeds such as pumpkin, hemp, flax, and chia are rich in omega 3 fats, so experiment with incorporating them into your diet. Sesame seeds and sunflower seeds are other good choices, and can also be ground into butters, the former becoming tahini. A note of caution: flax and chia seeds should be ground to avoid intestinal problems.

Drink Water

Dizziness, disorientation, and feelings of faintness are symptoms of panic, but they can also be signs of dehydration. A rule of thumb: drink half your body weight in ounces each day.

Experiment with Green Smoothies and Soups

If you can't consume 13 servings of vegetables a day, consider green smoothies. These drinks can provide a perfect blend of protein, fats, fruits, and vegetables and may solve the "What do I eat for breakfast?" problem. Check out Elyse Wagner's book *Smoothie Secrets Revealed* (2014), as it contains yummy smoothie recipes accompanied by healing words of wisdom. My basic smoothie recipe can be found in Appendix II.

Soups can be another good option. When my daughters were little, I disguised all types of vegetables in pureed soups. Bone broth

STEP 8

promotes good digestion, and what heals the gut, heals the mind. I've provided a recipe in Appendix II.

Eat Slowly and Chew Your Food

You can prepare the most nutritionally balanced meal, but if you're gulping it down in a hurry, not taking the time to chew it properly, multi-tasking while eating, overeating, or eating for reasons other than hunger, then you're stressing your system.

Eating quickly and not taking the time to properly chew and taste your food leads to incomplete digestion, which can be a significant source of chronic stress. Digestion begins in the mouth, where pre-digestion must occur to prevent partially digested food from passing through the intestines, subsequently fermenting and causing gas, bloating, and inadequate absorption of nutrients. As a rule of thumb, chew your food at least 25 times before swallowing it; 40 times would be even better!

Eat Regularly throughout the Day

How meals are timed throughout the day matters. Are you running out of the house without breakfast, skipping lunch, or coming home famished and eating a large meal late at night? If so, your adrenal glands aren't happy. The body, including your brain, constantly needs energy from blood sugar, even while asleep. By going for extended periods of time without eating and getting too hungry, blood sugar levels drop, which creates stress and taxes the adrenal glands.

To maintain a balanced state throughout the day, follow these guidelines: eat breakfast; have a snack to balance blood sugar and insulin levels; consume your biggest meal early in the day, make dinner the lightest meal, and stop eating three hours before bedtime. Alternatively, you may experience the most wellbeing by eating a late-morning breakfast, a large mid-afternoon lunch, a light dinner, avoiding snacks, and not eating from dinner until breakfast the next day (preferably a 12-hour fast). Experiment to determine which option works best for you. You may find that you need to eat every two to three hours when you initiate a "sugar detox." As your body adjusts and insulin resistance lessens, you may feel your best with slightly longer spans between meals.

Eat Mindfully

Just as important to consider as what, how, and when you're eating is why you're eating, which may be the most difficult pattern to change. When anxious, you may turn to food, and chances are you're not turning to broccoli or kale. Instead, you're likely reaching for a comfort food, usually some combination of sugar, salt, and fat. Are you using snack foods or sweets as a major form of stress reduction? Are you eating without awareness and subsequently eating so much that you feel stuffed and bloated?

Make eating a calming, relaxing experience. Use all of the tools we've focused on to dine with mindfulness. Begin by breathing slowly, and with your belly, as you approach a meal and imagine the blend of life-sustaining nutrients you'll be taking in. Warm your heart with gratitude for the food that's in front of you. Distract yourself from disturbing thoughts and sensations by maintaining awareness of the food you're eating, including the array of colors, aromas, textures, shapes, and tastes on your plate. Apply moment-by-moment awareness to chewing and swallowing. As you continue to belly breathe, observe how your stomach feels. Notice when you're beginning to feel full, a sensation you may not notice if you're eating too fast.

Approaching meals in a calm manner, eating slowly and mindfully, and refraining from combining meals with other activities, leads to parasympathetic dominance. Remember that proper digestion takes place when the sympathetic alarm system shuts off

STEP 8

and the relaxation response takes over. Likewise, the more efficient the digestive process, the calmer and more balanced you'll feel.

PUTTING TOGETHER STEPS 1 THROUGH 8

In Step 8, incorporate a new medicine: food. Remove the processed "food-like substances" that create imbalance and contribute to anxiety, and add foods that will act as the raw materials for creating health and inner peace.

Here's an example of how to integrate Steps 1 through 8:

Step 1:

* I won't fear these sensations; it's just panic.

Step 2:

* Scary thoughts and images about something being wrong triggered the alarm system.

Step 3:

* As I keep focusing on slow belly breathing, my body will stop thinking it's in danger and call off the alarm response.

Step 4:

* My muscles tightened up to allow me to fight or run away, so I'll turn my attention to unclenching.

Step 5:

* I can imagine a time when I felt relaxed and peaceful, remembering exactly where I was, what I was doing and what relaxation felt like.

STEP 8

Step 6:

- Panic feels uncomfortable, but I can cope with discomfort.

- So what if I feel tense all over, it's just proof that my alarm response works, and the false alarm will soon be over.

Step 7:

- While waiting patiently for the alarm system to shut off, I'll focus like a laser beam on something I truly enjoy.

Step 8:

- If I haven't eaten in a while, I'll have a snack with some protein and fat.

- I'll pay attention to what I've been eating in the past few days and set an intention to eat lots of vegetables, proteins and good fats.

- I'll eat the rainbow.

STEP 9
Use Nature's Medicine Chest

In Step 9 we turn to the use of vitamins, minerals, herbs, spices, and other supplements to help you develop and maintain inner quiet. Preparing healing foods or relaxing teas, experimenting with new spices, focusing on eliminating food triggers and environmental toxins, or obtaining herbal preparations or natural supplements have some elements in common. Besides being proactive, these engaging actions can also distract you from anxious feelings. Maybe you like the security of having an anti-anxiety medication handy. Just knowing that relief awaits you in a handy pill-form creates a calming effect. The "medications" described in this step can serve that function just as well.

Although obtaining all nutrients from food constitutes the ideal approach, often supplements are necessary as you're likely not getting all you need from diet alone. For example, if you don't eat fatty fish such as sardines, mackerel, anchovies, wild salmon, or herring on a frequent basis, then supplementing with fish oil makes sense. Likewise, even if you eat massive amounts of dark green vegetables every day, you might still be deficient in magnesium because the soil in which the greens were grown may be depleted in this important mineral.

Consider supplementing your diet to make up for any deficiencies that can't be overcome with dietary changes alone. But rather than rushing out to the store or going online to purchase a particular vitamin or mineral, I recommend consulting with a healthcare professional who has training in the use of nutritional supplements. He or she can advise you about dosage recommendations, drug-nutrient interaction effects, the specific time of day that's best to take particular supplements, which supplements should be taken together, which shouldn't be combined, and whether or not they should be taken on an empty stomach or with food. Another consideration involves the form of a particular supplement, for example, synthetic compared to natural, or tablet versus sublingual liquid. Keep in mind that deficiencies may not be related to how much you're ingesting, but rather to inadequate breakdown and absorption. A functional medicine practitioner can work with you to determine if this is the case.

If you've ever walked down a vitamin aisle in a store, then you know that determining which supplement to purchase can be confusing. Some brands add fillers, binders, sweeteners, and even artificial preservatives and coloring. If you work with a healthcare professional trained in nutrition, integrative, or functional medicine, they'll direct you to highly reputable nutraceutical companies. Although a prescription isn't required to obtain their products, you'll need to purchase these high-quality supplements from a licensed healthcare professional.

VITAMINS AND MINERALS

Here's a list of the top supplements for anxiety:

Magnesium

Looking for a stress antidote? Start with magnesium, one of the most powerful relaxation and anti-anxiety agents. Magnesium ensures the proper functioning of the nervous system, as well as the conversion of carbohydrates, proteins, and fats into energy. Magnesium reduces glutamate excitation in the brain and, as an added benefit, reduces the muscular irritability often associated with anxiety, therefore promoting a calming effect. Low magnesium significantly reduces the body's ability to relax and fall into a deep sleep.

Although needs increase during highly stressful times, deficiencies in this mineral may be reaching epidemic proportions, as the typical highly processed diet contains practically no magnesium. Sources of magnesium include dark green vegetables, sea vegetables, nuts, and beans, but our soil has become depleted over the years. Chronic stress and consumption of alcohol, salt, coffee, sugar, and phosphoric acid (found in soft drinks) decrease magnesium. Even more is lost through sweat, diuretics, and the use of antibiotics, or proton pump inhibitors (acid blockers commonly prescribed for GERD, or acid reflux).

Given the challenges of getting enough magnesium from foods alone, consider supplementing this mineral. Magnesium glycinate and magnesium citrate are safe and highly absorbable forms. Liquid magnesium is also available, which can be a good option for children. Magnesium, a.k.a. "nature's Valium," can be taken about one hour before bedtime to promote a good night's sleep. The dosage range is generally between 250 and 500 mg. It's best to take it on an empty stomach.

B-Complex

Think of B vitamins as the "anti-stress vitamins." They help the brain transform amino acids into neurotransmitters such as serotonin, norepinephrine, and dopamine, and can help keep cortisol levels within a normal range throughout the day. Vitamin B1 (thiamine), B2 (riboflavin), B3 (niacin), and B9 (folate) play a role in the process of abstract thinking.

A deficiency in vitamin B6 (pyradoxine) has been linked to hyperventilation and panic. Supplementing with B6 has been shown to elevate levels of GABA, the inhibitor neurotransmitter. If you're considering taking just B6, as opposed to a B-complex, up to 40 mg

STEP 9

taken twice a day is the recommended dosage. Check with your healthcare provider to make sure that this intervention is appropriate for your needs.

Stress depletes your store of B vitamins. Also keep in mind that certain medications such as acid-blockers and antidepressants further deplete B12, essential for energy production. Occasionally, supplementation with B12 may provoke an anxiety reaction, most likely due to a genetic variant. This remote possibility is one more reason to work with a knowledgeable healthcare professional.

It's generally best to begin with a low dose and work up slowly. I prefer taking B vitamins early in the day, as they can be energizing. Choose quality brands that use active forms of these nutrients. Look for folate in the form of 5-methyltetrahydrofolic acid and pyridozal-5-phosphate, the activated form of B6. Avoid synthetics, commonly found in cheaper, bargain brands. These products may also contain unwanted fillers, binders, and artificial coloring.

Fish Oils

Are you eating wild salmon, mackerel, anchovies, herring, or sardines at least several times a week? Probably not, so it's wise to supplement with fish oil to obtain a sufficient amount of omega 3 fatty acids, the brain food discussed earlier.

Make sure the product you choose is molecularly distilled, as contaminants such as heavy metals have been found in some brands. Although there's no set rule regarding dosages, adults usually begin with 1000 mg per day and work up to 2000 mg, although higher amounts have been suggested for short-term use (typically around 4000 mg per day in divided doses). Again, work with a functional medicine practitioner to determine how much fish oil is best for you. This is particularly important if you're considering therapeutic dosages, as in very high amounts there's some concern that the fats can oxidize, so other fats (vitamin E as mixed tocopherols and borage oil) need to be added to prevent this occurrence.

STEP 9

Vitamin C

Vitamin C, generally regarded as a potent antioxidant that stimulates the immune system and promotes wound healing, also wards off some of the detrimental effects of stress by lowering cortisol levels. Even a slight deficiency may result in an elevation of cortisol, which may lead to feeling "wired."

Vitamin D

Related to regulation of the immune system, cell health, and mood, vitamin D (which is actually a hormone) may indirectly affect anxiety levels. There's a strong probability that your body isn't making enough of this key hormone because you're most likely not out in the sun for long hours at a time. When you do go outside on a sunny day, you probably wear sunscreen. As a result, you're probably vitamin D deficient. As you age, you also lose your abililty to make vitamin D. Levels should be checked regularly as part of routine blood work-ups with a 25 (OH) vitamin D test, and although there's some controversy as to what represents an ideal blood level and an appropriate dosage for supplementation, most experts recommend 2000 IU (International Units) for adults and 1000 IU for children.

Other Important Vitamins and Minerals

Although I've only highlighted the importance of a few key vitamins and minerals, others to keep in mind are iron, zinc, copper, selenium, potassium, and calcium. All are critical for optimum health and the maintenance of a balanced state. Taking a good quality multi-vitamin supplement can provide insurance against deficits. One note of caution: postmenopausal women should not be taking supplemental iron unless advised to do so by a healthcare professional.

STEP 9

THE POWER OF SPICES

If food is medicine, then spices are some of the most potent medicines available. Contrary to the popular belief that spices make foods "hot," most spices are aromatic, not fiery. Healers have used them for medicinal purposes for thousands of years. Sanskrit writings from India 3000 years ago and ancient medical texts from China describe the many therapeutic uses of spices. Recently, studies on animal populations have been conducted in India and Asia to validate the effects of specific spices on cortisol levels. Experiment with a variety of spices, but keep in mind the importance of balance. A little may be good, but too much can be just as bad as none at all.

Following is a brief list of the spices associated with lowering anxiety. To learn more about these wonderful agents, refer to *Healing Spices* (2011) by Bharat Aggarwal, Ph.D.

Basil
According to researchers in India, several compounds in basil extract have anti-stress effects and may help to nourish the adrenal glands and normalize cortisol levels.

Coriander
One of the world's oldest spices, coriander has traditionally been recommended for relief of anxiety and insomnia. In animal studies it's been shown to act as a sedative and muscle relaxant.

Lavender
According to advocates of aromatherapy, the system of healing which uses the aromatic essences of plant oils called essential oils, the scent of lavender is said to be calming and can help promote sleep. Try a drop rubbed into each wrist. A note of caution: when using essential

STEP 9

oils, make sure to get 100 percent pure plant oils, as many products contain a blend of synthetic oils.

Lemongrass

Referred to as "the calming spice," lemongrass is often made into a tea. Native Brazilians drink *abaafado* to reduce anxiety. As an essential oil, it's wonderful to inhale.

Mint

In addition to aiding digestion, peppermint can lower anxiety. Try inhaling mint or using it as a refreshing tea.

Nutmeg

Traditional healers used nutmeg for a variety of conditions, including anxiety. More recently, an animal study in India confirmed its benefits as an anti-anxiety agent.

Rosemary

According to ancient healers, rosemary has special anti-anxiety powers. It was often used to treat dizziness. Just breathing rosemary scent can reduce cortisol levels.

- Soak a small cotton ball with rosemary essential oil.

- Wrap the cotton ball in a piece of cloth.

- Sniff the cloth to induce a calming effect.

Saffron

Saffron has a long history of use for anxiety and insomnia in traditional medicine. It's thought to have anti-inflammatory and antioxidant effects. Several animal studies demonstrated that saffron reduced anxiety-like activity, and one human study found that simply smelling saffron reduced anxiety. Begin using saffron as a tea, but if you're interested in a capsule form, check with an informed healthcare professional regarding dosage and side effects. If you're pregnant or have been diagnosed with bipolar disorder, saffron supplements are contraindicated.

Sage

Sage is another spice that's been used for thousands of years by Chinese medicine practitioners, Indian physicians, healers in ancient Greece, and by Native American tribes. Now there's research that demonstrates sage's ability to improve mood and reduce anxiety. Start by making sage tea, typically one teaspoon of dried sage and one cup of hot water. Sage leaf is also available in capsule form and the recommended dosage is 600 mg. Do not use sage if you're pregnant.

HERBS AS MEDICINE

Do you need more than relaxation techniques and calming foods and spices? Maybe you've chosen the "no medication" route but don't yet trust your ability to relax and aren't ready, willing, or able to use food as medicine. Maybe you're still experiencing panic and anxiety despite the use of supplemental vitamins, minerals, and fish oils. Consider the use of herbs.

Herbs as teas or herbal infusions are the mildest, gentlest delivery forms, so if you're new to herbs, begin here. Although commercially prepared tea bags may be more convenient, I prefer buying herbs in

STEP 9

bulk from reputable sources and then making a tea or preparing an herbal infusion. Just the act of preparing tea can have a calming effect.

- Use 1–3 tablespoons of dried herb(s) for each cup of water, or 4–8 tablespoons per quart.

- Pour boiling water over the herbs and steep for about 5 minutes.

- Strain and enjoy.

An herbal infusion consists of a large amount of a particular herb that's brewed for a longer period of time than a tea.

- Place about 1 cup of dried herb in a quart jar.

- Fill the jar to the top with hot water.

- Place the lid on tightly and steep for 4–10 hours.

- Strain and drink the liquid.

- Refrigerate the remainder.

Because quality and potency of herbs vary considerably, look for organic products from a reputable company.

Learning about herb–drug interaction effects is crucial and, as with prescription medications, the same precautions regarding pregnancy must be taken into consideration. Work with a qualified healthcare professional to address these issues. Just as you want to be aware of hidden food and spice sensitivities, it's also important to take into account the possibility that you may have an underlying sensitivity or intolerance to particular herbs.

It's best to begin with the mildest herbs with the strongest safety records. Here, in order of preference, is a listing of the herbs to consider for reducing anxiety:

STEP 9

Lemon Balm

Referred to as the "gladden herb," lemon balm is a mild anxiolytic that helps with restlessness and agitation, and can also enhance mood. Because most of the beneficial features come from the essential oils, a tea made from fresh leaves works best. Homegrown lemon balm, which grows well in partial sunlight, offers more potency than store-bought. Gather lemon balm before it flowers to preserve the fragrant, lemony taste and avoid bitterness.

- Add a handful of fresh or dried leaves to 1 cup of boiling water.

- Let it steep for about 5–10 minutes and strain.

If you prefer a liquid tincture, the standard recommendation calls for 1–5 droppers up to three times a day.

Lemon balm can be taken at bedtime for insomnia but doesn't induce sleepiness if taken during the day. If you're feeling stressed and anxious, the ritual of preparing and drinking lemon balm tea offers a soothing distraction. Just smelling the citrus scent can produce a relaxation effect.

Passionflower

I'm crazy about passionflower! This mild, but powerful herb increases GABA, the inhibitory neurotransmitter in the central nervous system. There's evidence that passionflower compares favorably to certain anti-anxiety medications. It can act as a mild sedative and may be particularly helpful if you have difficulty falling asleep due to racing thoughts.

To work up slowly, start with a passionflower tea. If you want to try a tincture, the typical recommended dosage is one dropperful in a little warm water. Passionflower also comes in capsule form. Work up to two capsules of the extract, up to four times a day as needed, or around 300–400 mg per day. Although considered safe for children, passionflower should be avoided during pregnancy.

STEP 9

Skullcap

A delicate wildflower, skullcap has been used for centuries to induce a relaxed state. It can be prepared as a tea or taken as a tincture or capsule. Because this herb has a bitter taste, try blending it with mint to mask the taste if you want to use it in tea form. Skullcap may have sedating effects, especially for those with depression in addition to anxiety. It's reported to be safe for children.

Because passionflower combines well with skullcap and lemon balm, consider using this combination for reducing panic sensations. Blend these herbs for a soothing tea.

- Combine equal parts of dried passionflower, skullcap, lemon balm, and spearmint (for flavor).

- Steep 1 tablespoon of the mixture for 15 minutes in 1 cup of hot water.

- Strain well.

If making this tea during daytime hours, use less passionflower and skullcap, as they're more sedating than lemon balm.

Motherwort

Motherwort offers fast relief from panic attacks as it calms a rapid heartbeat. Fortunately, this herb grows easily in most gardens. Unfortunately, it's very bitter as a tea but can be blended with other herbs. Motherwort should not be used during pregnancy.

Hops

Used to brew beer in Europe since the eleventh century, hops act as a sedative and anxiolytic that can both induce sleep and improve the quality of sleep. It's typically combined with valerian. Some nutraceutical companies offer products that contain a mixture of valerian, hops, and passionflower.

Kava

Kava is native to the South Pacific, where it was traditionally used as an intoxicating herb for ceremonies. Natives of this region used kava tea for centuries to promote relaxation, as in small doses it produces a quieting effect and acts as a muscle relaxant. Taken as a fresh root tincture, a fast-acting form, it usually has noticeable effects within minutes. As with lemon balm, kava doesn't have a sedative effect when taken during the day, but can promote sleep when taken at bedtime.

This herb earned a bad reputation when reports of liver toxicity surfaced several years ago. However, the problem occurred because some manufacturers, eager to cut costs, used the above ground parts of kava in their preparations rather than the root. Make sure you purchase kava root, not just kava, and only buy from a reputable supplier.

Although not considered to be addictive, little is known about its long-term effects, therefore kava should only be used for short-term support (no longer than three months at a time) and preferably on an intermittent rather than a daily basis. The usual recommendation is one dropperful of liquid tincture in warm water as needed, up to three times a day. As with other herbs, it should not be taken with alcohol, during pregnancy, or if liver disease is present. If you're considering the use of kava, I strongly recommend consulting with a healthcare professional who has experience working with this herb for anxiety.

Valerian

Popular as far back as Roman times, valerian was known for both its anxiety-reducing and sleep-inducing properties. As mentioned earlier, some supplement manufacturers combine valerian with other calming herbs, such as hops and passionflower. It's not recommended for children, should not be taken during pregnancy, and should not be combined with alcohol, sedatives, or antidepressant medication. As with the other herbs we've been discussing, seek the advice of an experienced practitioner to determine if valerian is appropriate for you.

Adaptogens

Adaptogens are a class of herbs that have been used for thousands of years to reduce the effects of chronic stress and restore balance to the adrenal glands. In short, adaptogens help the body adapt to stress. All adaptogens are relatively safe, with no evidence of toxicity but, as with any substance, can be harmful if misused or taken in extremely high doses.

Perhaps the most well known are the ginsengs: Asian or Panax ginseng, American ginseng, and Siberian ginseng. These herbs help the body fight fatigue and physical exhaustion due to chronic stress but, because they may increase cortisol levels, they may be contraindicated for acute anxiety.

Many adaptogens come from Ayurvedic medicine, the 5000-year-old Indian healing system loosely translated from Sanskrit as "life knowledge or science." According to Ayurvedic tradition, "what heals also prevents." Herbs effective in treating specific conditions can also serve as a "food," providing targeted nourishment to specific physiological systems. For example, turmeric, popularized for its anti-inflammatory properties, can also be eaten as a culinary spice. I purchase turmeric root and add it to my morning smoothie.

Adaptogens typically have multiple rather than single effects and are seldom used in isolation. Instead, they're combined in formulas designed to balance and harmonize the properties of the constituent herbs. Pairing of herbs illustrates the concept of synergy, as each may have a mild effect, but two or three together act more effectively to create change.

STEP 9

PANAX GINSENG

This adaptogen increases energy and the ability to deal with stress. Although generally considered to be safe, it's not recommended for individuals with hypertension or hypoglycemia. Continuous use for more than about three months is also contraindicated.

ASHWAGANDHA

Loosely translated as "strength of a horse" and sometimes referred to as Indian ginseng, ashwagandha increases energy and stamina while also promoting a calming and muscle-relaxing effect. It can be a good choice for those suffering from a combination of chronic anxiety, fatigue, and insomnia. While there are no reports of adverse side effects, it shouldn't be combined with alcohol and other sedatives or taken during pregnancy.

Ashwagandha is typically recommended in doses of 500 mg once or twice daily, before meals. As with all herbs, start with the smallest dose and work up gradually. Responses are typically seen within 2–4 weeks of regular use.

HOLY BASIL

Also referred to as tulsi, holy basil can restore balance to the adrenal glands. In India, expect to find holy basil growing in the garden of every family that practices Ayurvedic healing. It's a powerful antioxidant and anti-inflammatory agent that promotes relaxation and protects against the stress response. Look for holy basil as a tea and a concentrated extract.

GOTU KOLA

An herb used for hundreds of years in Indian and Chinese medicine, gotu kola can reduce symptoms of stress, anxiety, and depression. Although it may help curb food cravings and urges to binge associated with stress, it may also raise blood sugar levels.

STEP 9

Because ashwagandha, gotu kola, and holy basil provide "calm energy," they work well for those who complain of feeling drained and exhausted due to their anxiety. Other adaptogens which may provide relief from anxiety are schisandra, reishi, and jiaogulan, herbs that have been used for centuries in Asia, and blue vervain, a little-known herb that can be combined with motherwort (one part blue vervain to two parts motherwort), skullcap, or ashwagandha. For a complete discussion of these and other adaptogens, one of the best guides to refer to is *Adaptogens: Herbs for Strength, Stamina, and Stress Relief* (2007), by David Winston and Steven Maimes. I also recommend consulting with a functional medicine practitioner or a medical professional with training in Ayurvedic medicine to determine whether or not you're a good candidate for adaptogens and, if so, which one, or which combination, would be most beneficial.

Still More Options from "Nature's Medicine Chest"
MELATONIN
Melatonin, a hormone produced by the pineal gland in the brain from the amino acid tryptophan, helps regulate sleep/wake cycles. Levels should be lowest during midday and highest at night, as daylight slows production while darkness increases it. Melatonin levels decrease with age. Take 1–5 mg about one hour before bedtime to help with sleep-onset insomnia and improve quality of sleep. The slow-release form may help prevent awakening in the middle of the night.

INOSITOL
Although the mechanism of action isn't entirely clear, there's an abundance of research to support the use of inositol, also known as vitamin B8, for the treatment of anxiety. This supplement has a naturally sweet taste and 5–10 grams per day can be used in powdered form. Consider taking inositol at bedtime, as it's been shown to reduce insomnia and promote a restful sleep.

STEP 9

L-THEANINE

An amino acid found in the leaves of green tea, l-theanine is known for its relaxation inducing effects and can also be used at night to promote sleep. Considered extremely safe, it's usually recommended in dosages of up to 200 mg per day, the equivalent of about four cups of green tea.

TAURINE

Taurine is an amino acid that has a powerful anti-anxiety effect since it can cross the blood–brain barrier to raise GABA levels. It can be taken in supplemental form. Start with a low dosage and build-up to 1000 mg twice a day.

GABA

If you suffer from panic, you may have low levels of GABA, an inhibitory neurotransmitter. Although GABA is available in supplement form, it doesn't cross the blood–brain barrier in any appreciable amount. Fortunately, natural agents exist that can travel to the brain and either act to enhance GABA or mimic GABA activity. Adding the necessary raw materials to the diet will raise levels. The amino acids taurine and l-theanine, vitamin B3, vitamin B6, vitamin B12, inositol, and magnesium all boost GABA production.

PHOSPHATIDYLSERINE

There's an abundance of research suggesting that high levels of the stress hormone cortisol are related to anxiety. Phosphatidylserine, a phospholipid chemical found in cell membranes, has been found to reduce cortisol. Available in supplement form, 300–400 mg per day is the recommended amount. An experienced healthcare professional can work with you to determine whether or not a trial of phosphatidylserine would be beneficial.

STEP 9

PUTTING TOGETHER STEPS 1 THROUGH 9

Now it's time to practice integrating what you've learned so far. Continue substituting or adding your own variations.

Step 1:

- It's just panic and you've been here before, so let go of "fearing fear."

Step 2:

- You've set off your alarm system with scary thoughts and now it's working exquisitely well to protect you from perceived danger.

Step 3:

- Start taking quiet belly breaths to begin the slow process of turning off the alarm system.

Step 4:

- Unclench your muscles, as they don't need to tighten up in preparation to fight or run away.

Step 5:

- Imagine one of the happiest days in your life.
- Imagine happiness right now.

Step 6:

- Repeat to yourself: "So what if I've worked myself up to a panic attack, the feelings are uncomfortable but not awful, horrible, or terrible" and "I can tolerate the panic and I'll soon feel better."

STEP 9

Step 7:

- While waiting for the panic to pass, find an engaging distraction, especially humor or enjoyable movement.

- To drain away every last ounce of tension, settle into Child's Pose.

Step 8:

- Pay attention to what you're putting into your body and set an intention to remove the "bad stuff."

- Boost your brain health by eating vegetables, proteins, healthy fats, and a rainbow of color.

- Eat slowly and mindfully.

Step 9:

- Work with a knowledgeable practitioner to determine if you have nutritional deficiencies.

- Use supplemental forms of vitamins, minerals, and fish oils from reputable companies, as recommended by your healthcare practitioner.

- Open nature's medicine chest to discover the healing power of herbs and spices.

STEP 9

STEP 10
Embrace Your Character Strengths

Personal stories involving triumph over panic showcase heroism as great as that depicted in films, plays, and novels. Over the years, I've been privileged to witness many such journeys and transformations from fearfulness to hardiness. Just like a hardy plant that refuses to be blown over by a strong wind, hardy individuals withstand whatever stressor comes their way. Resiliency and hardiness, which trump fearfulness and panic, can be cultivated.

To build-up resiliency, access your character strengths and virtues. That involves turning to positive psychology, a field of study that looks at optimal functioning and the factors that contribute to flourishing. Pioneered by Martin Seligman and Mihalyi Csikszentmihalyi, positive psychology focuses on what's best about human beings, and what's best are their strengths and virtues. I want you to nurture what's best, not attempt to fix what's broken. That's why Step 10 is about using your character strengths.

You may have heard of the *Diagnostic and Statistical Manual of Mental Disorders*, the psychiatric manual that classifies what's wrong with you. As you've learned by now, I believe there's a better way of looking at symptoms. That's why in Step 10 we're turning to *Character Strengths and Virtues* (2004) by Chris Peterson and Martin Seligman, the manual of the "sanities" that classifies what's right with you. Rather than "happiology," positive psychology integrates all aspects of the human experience, the positive as well as the negative.

Signature strengths are stable, universal personality traits that are the foundational building blocks of human goodness and flourishing. They're the essence of wellbeing. Through both empirical and historical analysis, 24 strengths have been identified and these are grouped into six virtues: wisdom, courage, humanity, justice, temperance, and transcendence. You possess every one of these strengths, but some may stand out as your key character strengths. If you're curious as to what these might be, go to www.viacharacter.org and take the character strengths survey online.

By acknowledging and using your character strengths, you'll be able to continue practicing the previous 9 steps outlined in this book. These strengths are your keys to letting go of anxiety for good and attaining optimal wellbeing. Here are some suggestions for how to begin recognizing and using your strengths:

- Start a strengths diary.

- Select a period of time, such as 7 days, and for each of these 7 days jot down examples of how you used your strengths to overcome worries, fear, panic, or negative thinking.

Check out a sample strengths diary in Appendix III.

YOUR 24 CHARACTER STRENGTHS
The Virtue of Wisdom
The strengths grouped under wisdom entail the acquisition and use of knowledge. Just imagining that you can trust your inner wisdom will induce a calming response.

CREATIVITY
Think of ways you've used ingenuity or thought of creative solutions to problems. Whenever you practice mindfulness, you're opening

STEP 10

yourself up to the possibility of finding creativity. Can you remember times in the past when you used creativity to deal with a difficult situation?

CURIOSITY

If you've ever experienced a desire to increase your knowledge, learn something new, or take an active interest in an ongoing experience, then you've displayed your curiosity strength. Just by reading this book you've exhibited curiosity. Can you practice experiencing the world around you with a beginner's mind and breakthrough mindless patterns and routines? Mindfulness and curiosity go hand in hand and together will lessen anxiety.

JUDGMENT

When you practice thinking like a scientist, you're using the strength of judgment. That means employing logic, reason, rationality, and open-mindedness rather than "catastrophizing" and jumping to illogical conclusions. When you find yourself worrying or panicking, can you play devil's advocate with yourself or recognize that you're using tunnel vision? Practice using your judgment strength and notice how much calmer you feel.

LOVE OF LEARNING

Do you enjoy learning for the sake of learning? As you progressed through the 10 steps, did you experience positive feelings when you mastered a new skill? Would you like to rekindle a hobby or interest you used to be passionate about or learn a new one so as to distract you from anxiety? If so, then you're accessing your love of learning.

PERSPECTIVE

As you continue to practice letting go of panic and anxiety, access the perspective strength that's part of thinking like a scientist. You possess the ability to make sound judgments about what's important

STEP 10

in life. When you're upsetting yourself, how about remembering the wise decisions you've made in the past? Access your inner wisdom to put worries into perspective.

The Virtue of Courage

If you're familiar with the classic movie, *The Wizard of Oz*, then you know that the cowardly lion seeking courage possessed that virtue all along. I often tell my clients to find their inner courage and "be brave."

BRAVERY

Overcoming panic and anxiety involves acts of bravery. Reflect on times in the past when you voluntarily showed your bravery strength. Can you be brave enough to stop "fearing fear"? How about deploying "20 seconds of courage" the next time you're feeling scared?

PERSEVERANCE

Perseverance is one of the strengths most associated with good health and authentic happiness. How many times have you continued on despite challenges? Can you practice your perseverance strength by enlisting optimism and visualizing yourself as relaxed and panic-free rather than giving up and telling yourself you'll never get better?

HONESTY

When you accept "what is" change happens. When you accept anxiety, you're being honest with yourself and accepting yourself just as you are right now. As a result, you're embracing authenticity and being genuine, thus acting with integrity and on your way to finding wellbeing. Can you combine bravery and perseverance with your honesty strength? In other words, acknowledge fear, but do it anyway.

STEP 10

ZEST

Vitality, vigor, excitement, energy, and enthusiasm are all words that describe zest. This character strength is most connected with a life of pleasure, engagement, and meaning. I encourage clients to call low-level anxiety excitement. Notice when you feel charged up and full of energy. Often it's before a big event that could also be anxiety-provoking. Rather than calling these feelings anxiety, experiment with changing the label to excitement and notice how this switch makes a difference. Explore the many possibilities for living life with zest. Whenever you engage in an activity with complete mindfulness, share positive experiences or simply enjoy a slow belly breath, you have an opportunity to feel zest.

The Virtue of Humanity

While the humanity strengths are interpersonal and involve tending to and befriending others, I'd like you to consider turning these strengths inward as well.

LOVE

Compassionate love centers on caring for others (significant others, parents, children, friends, pets) and living a life that emphasizes commitment. But too much tending and befriending can be stressful. Can you incorporate self-love by committing to practicing these 10 steps?

KINDNESS

Kindness implies showing generosity, nurturance, care, compassion, or just plain niceness. What about self-compassion? Can you turn your kindness strength inward? Can you soothe yourself? Can you practice saying no?

STEP 10

SOCIAL INTELLIGENCE

Social intelligence refers to recognizing feelings, cues, motives, and signals, both within you and in others. How quickly can you identify the unpleasant sensations associated with anxiety? After you recognize them, how quickly can you use the 10 steps to delete them? If your thoughts lead to negative emotions, ask yourself if these feelings are helpful. Do they motivate you or limit you?

The Virtue of Justice

The justice strengths underlie healthy community life. Being part of a community fosters wellbeing and your ability to thrive.

TEAMWORK

Do you enjoy working with others and contributing to a group? If you believe that you're an integral part of a larger social whole, consider the many possibilities that teamwork offers for distracting you from anxiety. How can you use your teamwork strength to move away from the isolation of the "I" in illness? Where can you find community life that fosters the "we" in wellness? Do you want to share insights and receive support from others who are also using the 10 Step Program? Join my Stop Panicking Facebook group through the Feed Your Mind Wellness Facebook page or through www.feedyourmindwellness.com.

FAIRNESS

Keep in mind that your character strengths can also work against you. If you have a strong sense of social justice and a caring, compassionate nature, then you may have difficulty accepting what isn't fair. Can you practice letting go of "should," as in "this shouldn't be happening," or "he or she shouldn't be acting this way"?

STEP 10

LEADERSHIP

When you take these 10 steps to overcome panic, your demeanor changes. You'll exhibit a quiet strength and others will take notice. When you're calm, grateful, and deeply mindful of the world around you, the electromagnetic signals emanating from your heart change and those around you will sense it. You'll be using your leadership strength to produce a quieting response in someone else. Furthermore, if you share your story of how you overcame panic, you'll inspire others to follow your lead. That's another reason why I encourage you to join our Facebook group through Feed Your Mind Wellness.

The Virtue of Temperance

Anxiety may take the form of excessive worrying and catastrophic thinking. It may also lead to overeating or emotional eating. Use your temperance strengths to protect you against these excesses.

FORGIVENESS

First and foremost, practice self-forgiveness. Along with accepting the shortcomings of others and letting go of anger, recriminations, and resentment, use your forgiveness strength to pardon yourself for feeling nervous, overreacting, acting fearfully, or working yourself up to a full-blown panic attack. Practice forgiveness if you make a poor food choice or overeat.

HUMILITY

Can you accurately assess your abilities and recognize your limitations? Practicing humility leads to being open to new ideas, and that ensures success in overcoming panic. In other words, let go of the irrational statement, "I have to," as in "I have to do it perfectly," or "I have to completely stop panicking."

STEP 10

PRUDENCE

Considered the mother of all strengths, prudence implies using reason to guide behavior, weighing risks against benefits, and avoiding excess. If there's a silver lining in suffering from anxiety, it may be that you have an overabundance of prudence. There's value in acting cautiously and avoiding risky behaviors. If anxiety causes you to spend a lot of time considering the consequences of engaging in a particular behavior or making a decision, embrace your anxiety and label yourself as cautious. Sure I had a lot of fears during my childhood and adolescent years, but what were the advantages of not being a dare devil?

SELF-REGULATION

Think of self-regulation as the ability to control your thoughts, actions, and feelings. It's considered to be one of the most important character strengths because exercising self-control blunts the deleterious effects of stress and trauma. The more you practice the 10 steps, the better you'll become at self-regulating how you think, what you feel, and how you respond to challenging people and situations. The mind–body techniques that you've been learning are referred to as self-regulation strategies.

The Virtue of Transcendence

In order to truly thrive, you need a sense of purpose or deeper meaning in your life. The transcendence strengths have to do with finding meaning or establishing a connection that goes beyond interpersonal relationships. When you access these strengths, you'll experience a profound sense of inner peace.

APPRECIATION OF BEAUTY AND EXCELLENCE

Discover the goodness, beauty and excellence around you. When you practice mindfulness, the opportunity awaits to become filled

STEP 10

with awe, wonder, admiration, amazement, and elevation. For example, when you tune in to your body's natural ability to create a quiet state, appreciate the power of your remarkable relaxation response.

GRATITUDE

Experiencing gratitude creates a strong healing response. It significantly lessens anxiety, improves mood, lessens physical symptoms, and leads to better sleep. How many ways can you express thankfulness and affirm that life is good? Can you turn "stressings" into blessings?

HOPE

Hope correlates closely with happiness. Even if you're still experiencing panic and anxiety, if you maintain hope that you'll get better, than you've already started a healing response. When you have a setback, remember that when one door closes, another door opens. Use your hope strength by practicing realistic optimism: leniency for the past, appreciation of the moment, and opportunity seeking for the future.

HUMOR

Humor is one of the character strengths most associated with the pleasure pathway to happiness. Laughter helps you overcome despair. As stated before, it's impossible to laugh and feel anxious at the same time. During the height of an anxiety attack, access your humor strength and ask yourself: "What would a comedian say?"

SPIRITUALITY

While spirituality can refer to beliefs about a higher purpose or a quest for existential meaning, it can also be interpreted as an inner journey leading to transformation. Use each moment as an opportunity to

STEP 10

connect with what's precious. Do so by incorporating all of your character strengths. The result: a calm, peaceful state.

ACCESS YOUR CHARACTER STRENGTHS TO CREATE LASTING CHANGE

The ingredients to create permanent change are inside you: character strengths combined with your body's quieting response. Use your character strengths to unlock the treasure chest of resources that turn off the alarm system, thereby stopping a panic attack and deleting anxiety. Think of these tools as powerful medicine, and with sustained, regular use, the structure and functioning of the brain changes in profound ways.

- Use your creativity, curiosity, good judgment, love of learning, and perspective to continue exploring ways to find inner peace.

- Bring forth your bravery, perseverance, honesty, and zest to courageously stop "fearing fear" and fully embrace life.

- Call upon your capacity to love, express kindness, and exhibit social intelligence to warm your heart as you care for yourself and others.

- Use teamwork, leadership skills, and your sense of fairness to overcome obstacles that contribute to anxiety.

- Practice using the temperance strengths of forgiveness, humility, prudence, and self-regulation to control irrational thoughts and fears.

- Find your appreciation of beauty and excellence, gratitude, hope, humor, and spirituality to change an anxiety response to a peaceful state and profoundly heal yourself.

STEP 10

Think of your character strengths as the keys to your wellbeing. They unlock your potential to fully experience what all human beings need to thrive: positive emotions, full engagement (mindfulness), fulfilling relationships, meaning or purpose, and mastery or achievement. Positive psychologists refer to these components of wellbeing by the acronym PERMA.

When you embrace your strengths on a daily basis you're producing a physiological healing response and preventing the onset of anxiety. If panic develops, call upon your positive strengths of character so that you can practice the previous 9 steps with ease. Continue to practice and you'll achieve permanent change. Continue to put in the good stuff that your body wants and take out the bad stuff that's not serving you. When you incorporate the 10 steps into your daily life, you're giving yourself the most powerful combination of ingredients for stopping panic and letting go of anxiety.

PUTTING ALL 10 STEPS TOGETHER

Step 1:

- ◆ Recognize that you're not physically or mentally ill and stop "fearing fear."

Step 2:

- ◆ Realize that negative thoughts and images turned on your alarm system, your body is doing a good job to protect you from what it believes is real danger, but the alarm system shuts off very slowly.

Step 3:

- ◆ Begin to turn off the false alarm by taking slow belly breaths.

STEP 10

Step 4:

- Sit or stand tall and unclench tight muscles.

Step 5:

- Imagine feeling relaxed and pretend you're in a wonderful place filled with positive sights and sounds while you warm your heart with feelings of joy and gratitude.

Step 6:

- Detect catastrophic thoughts and think like a scientist to arrive at a more rational conclusion.

Step 7:

- Find something to enjoy, someone to be with, or something to laugh at that'll grab your complete attention and distract you.

Step 8:

- Eat calming foods and prevent future anxiety by removing inflammatory foods and reducing toxic load.

Step 9:

- Use spices and herbs to create a calming response and take the right supplements to prevent nutritional deficiencies.

Step 10:

- Believe that you possess the character strengths to overcome panic and anxiety and use them every day to create wellbeing.

By successfully coping with life's difficulties and using obstacles as opportunities to use your character strengths, you're building hardiness. Rather than viewing panic and anxiety as negatives, view them from a different perspective: opportunities to practice

STEP 10

mindfulness, accept all of life's experiences, gain a better self-perception, and laugh at yourself. As you continue to find balance and develop greater resilience, anticipate a time when you'll look back on panic attacks and worrisome thoughts and see them as the vehicles that brought you into a state of good health.

Practicing the 10 Easy Steps Leads to Optimal Wellness

Use the 10 steps as a starting point for discovering balance, strength, and inner quiet, but view your journey as a work in progress. Trusting creativity and mindfulness, you'll continually find additional ways of creating internal stillness. The more you incorporate slow belly breaths, positive images, realistic thinking, and enjoyable movement, plus the more you add calming foods and positive connections to your life, the greater the opportunity for achieving a state of harmony. Applying this functional medicine-based model to understanding and managing panic and anxiety has the potential to balance brain chemistry. But functional medicine recognizes the interconnectedness of all parts of you. As a consequence of practicing these 10 steps, you'll create profound changes in all the other systems of your body as well. Do you need to improve your digestion, strengthen your immune response, sleep more soundly, heal your cardiovascular system, balance your hormones, or beef up your ability to excrete toxins? If so, continue practicing these 10 Easy Steps to find vitality and total wellness.

STEP 10

APPENDIX I
Resources

SUPPORT TO STOP PANIC ATTACKS
IN 10 EASY STEPS
Feed Your Mind Wellness

www.feedyourmindwellness.com

PANIC AND ANXIETY
Harris, D. (2014) *10% Happier.* HarperCollins Publishers.

Ross, J. (1994) *Triumph over Fear.* Bantam.

Swede, S. and Jaffe, S. (2000) *The Panic Attack Recovery Book.* New American Library.

Wilson, R. (1986) *Don't Panic.* Harper and Row.

Anxiety and Depression Association of America

www.adaa.org

The tAPir Times (Anxiety Panic internet resource)

http://algy.com/anxiety/wordpress

MIND-BODY MEDICINE
Gordon, J. (2009) *Unstuck.* Penguin.

Gordon, J. (1996) *Manifesto for a New Medicine.* Perseus Books.

Hamilton, D. (2010) *How Your Mind Can Heal Your Body.* Hay House.

Minich, D. (2011) *Quantum Healing: An A–Z Guide for Over 100 Common Ailments.* Conari Press.

Pelletier, K. (1977) *Mind as Healer, Mind as Slayer.* Dell Publishing.

Rankin, L. (2013) *Mind over Medicine.* Hay House.

Remen, R. N. (2006) *Kitchen Table Wisdom.* Penguin Group.

Sapolsky, R. (2004) *Why Zebras Don't Get Ulcers.* St. Martin's Griffin.

Weil, A. (2011) *Spontaneous Happiness*. Little, Brown and Company.

Weil, A. (2000) *Spontaneous Healing*. Ballantine.

Arizona Center for Integrative Medicine

www.integrativemedicine.arizonacenter.edu

www.drweil.com

Center for Mind-Body Medicine

www.cmbm.org

www.jamesgordonmd.com

FUNCTIONAL MEDICINE

Bland, J. S. (2014) *The Disease Delusion*. HarperCollins.

Jones, D. S. (ed.) (2010) *Textbook of Functional Medicine*. Institute for Functional Medicine.

Wahls, T. (2014) *The Wahl's Protocol*. Penguin Group.

The Institute for Functional Medicine

www.functionalmedicine.org

UltraWellness Center

www.ultrawellness.com

www.drhyman.com

BREATHING

Fahri, D. (1996) *The Breathing Book*. Henry Holt and Co.

Fried, R. (1999) *Breathe Well, Be Well*. John Wiley & Sons.

Strom, M. (2010) *A Life Worth Breathing*. Skyhorse.

CD RECORDINGS ON BREATHING

Cohen, K. (2005) *Healthy Breathing*. Sounds True.

Weil, A. (1999) *Breathing: The Master Key to Self Healing*. Sounds True.

MUSCLE RELAXATION

Benson, H. (1975) *The Relaxation Response*. William Morrow.

McKay, M., Davis, M., Robbins Eshelman, E., and Fanning, P. (2008) *The Relaxation and Stress Reduction Workbook.* New Harbinger Publications.

Zemach-Bersin, D., Zemach-Bersin, K., and Reese, M. (1990) *Relaxercise.* Harper Collins.

HEART RATE VARIABILITY TRAINING

Childre, D. and Rozman, D. (2006) *Transforming Anxiety.* New Harbinger.

Childre, D., Martin, H., and Beech, D. (2000) *The HeartMath Solution.* HarperCollins.

Emwave Personal Trainer and Inner Balance

www.heartmath.org

IMAGERY

Naparstek, B. (1994) *Staying Well with Guided Imagery.* Warner Books.

Rossman, M. L. (2000) *Guided Imagery for Self-Healing: An Essential Resource for Anyone Seeking Wellness.* New World Library.

Sternberg, E. (2009) *Healing Spaces.* Belknap Press of Harvard University Press.

Academy for Guided Imagery

www.academyforguidedimagerycom

MINDFULNESS

Brantley, J. (2007) *Calming Your Anxious Mind.* New Harbinger Publications.

Csikszentmihalyi, M. (1990) *Flow.* Harper.

Kabot-Zinn, J. (1990) *Full-Catastrophe Living.* Dell.

Stahl, B., Goldstein, E., and Kabat-Zinn, J. (2010) *A Mindfulness-Based Stress Reduction Workbook.* New Harbinger Publications.

RATIONAL THINKING

Barlow, D. and Craske, M. (1989) *Mastery of Your Anxiety and Panic.* Graywind.

Burns, D. (1980) *The Feeling Good Handbook.* Penguin.

Ellis, A. (2006) *How to Stubbornly Refuse to Make Yourself Miserable about Anything: Yes Anything!* Citadel Press.

Ellis, A. (1998) *How to Control Your Anxiety Before It Controls You.* Citadel Press.

Ellis, A. (1975) *A New Guide to Rational Living.* Wilshire Book Company.

HUMOR

AFI's 100 Years, 100 Laughs (2000) American Film Institute. Available at www.afi.com/100years/laughs.

American School of Laughter Yoga
www.laughteryogaamerica.com
Laughter Yoga University
www.laughteryoga.org

YOGA

Forbes, B. (2011) *Yoga for Emotional Balance.* Shambhala Publications.

Lasater, J. (2011) *Relax and Renew: Restful Yoga for Stressful Times.* Rodmell Press.

NurrieStearns, M. and NurrieStearns, R. (2010) *Yoga for Anxiety.* New Harbinger Publications.

Yoga Journal
www.yogajournal.com
Yoga Finder
www.yogafinder.com

GUT HEALTH

Lipski, L. (2012) *Digestive Wellness, 4th ed.* McGraw Hill.

Mullin, G. E. and Swift, K. M. (2011) *The Inside Tract: Your Good Gut Guide to Great Digestive Health.* Rodale.

BRAIN HEALTH

Arden, J. B. (2010) *Rewire Your Brain.* John Wiley and Sons.

Hanson, R. (2009) *Buddha's Brain.* New Harbinger.

Hyman, M. (2009) *UltraMind Solution.* Scribner.

Perlmutter, D. and Villoldo, A. (2011) *Power Up Your Brain.* Hay House.

ENVIRONMENTAL TOXINS

Junger, A. (2012) *Clean.* HarperOne.

Environmental Working Group

www.ewg.org

FOOD AS MEDICINE

Hyman, M. (2014) *10-Day Detox Diet.* Little, Brown and Company.

Hyman, M. (2012) *The Blood Sugar Solution.* Little, Brown and Company.

Perlmutter, D. (2013) *Grain Brain: The Surprising Truth about Wheat, Carbs, and Sugar – Your Brain's Silent Killers.* Little, Brown and Company.

Pollan, M. (2010) *Food Rules: An Eater's Manual.* Penguin Books.

Food and Spirit

www.foodandspirit.com

HERBS AND SPICES

Aggarwal, B. (2011) *Healing Spices.* Sterling Publishing.

Gladstar, R. (2014) *Herbs for Stress and Anxiety.* Storey Publishing.

Murray, M. T. and Pizzorno, J. (2012) *The Encyclopedia of Natural Medicine, 3rd ed.* Atria Books.

Winston, D. and Maimes, S. (2007) *Adaptogens: Herbs for Strength, Stamina, and Stress Relief.* Healing Arts Press.

American Botanical Council

www.herbalgram.org

American Herbalist Guild

www.americanherbalistsguild.com

Herb Research Foundation

www.herbs.org

FAVORITE COOKBOOKS

Amsterdam, E. (2013) *Paleo Cooking from Elana's Pantry*. Ten Speed Press.

Katz, R. (2013) *The Longevity Kitchen*. Ten Speed Press.

Perlmutter, D. (2014) *The Grain Brain Cookbook: More than 150 Life-Changing Gluten-Free Recipes to Transform your Health*. Hachette Book Group.

Tam, M. and Fong, H. (2013) *Nom Nom Paleo*. Andrews McMeel Publishing.

Wagner, E. (2014) *Smoothie Secrets Revealed*. My Kitchen Shrink Inc.

Walker, D. (2013) *Against All Grain*. Victory Belt Publishing.

CHARACTER STRENGTHS

Niemiec, R. M. (2014) *Mindfulness and Character Strengths*. Hogrefe Publishing.

Peterson, C. and Seligman, M. (2004) *Character Strengths and Virtues: A Handbook and Classification*. Oxford University Press.

Seligman, M. (2011) *Flourish: A Visionary Understanding of Happiness and Well-being*. Free Press.

Seligman, M. (2002) *Authentic Happiness*. Free Press.

BIOFEEDBACK ORGANIZATIONS

Association of Applied Psychophysiology and Biofeedback (AAPB)
www.aapb.org

Biofeedback Certification International Alliance (BCIA)
www.bcia.org

APPENDIX II
Basic Recipes

CALMING GREEN SMOOTHIE
Ingredients

- 1 cup of a liquid, for example:

  - ► water
  - ► unsweetened organic almond milk
  - ► full fat organic coconut milk

  Experiment with other nut milks, such as hazelnut or cashew, or try hemp milk.

- 1 cup of organic greens (remove large center stems), for example:

  - ► romaine or other dark lettuce leaves
  - ► spinach
  - ► kale (tear off from center stem)
  - ► parsley
  - ► collard greens
  - ► Swiss chard
  - ► dandelion

  Choose one or combine several, but don't use the same type of greens every day:

- 1 cup of organic fruit (either fresh or frozen), for example:

  - ► blueberries
  - ► raspberries
  - ► strawberries
  - ► blackberries

- ► banana
- ► mango
- ► melon
- ► apple

For blood sugar control, limit fruit to ½ cup of berries.

Other options (experiment and use your creativity):

- ◆ 1 tbsp. ground flax seeds or chia seeds
- ◆ 1–3 tbsp. hemp seeds
- ◆ 1 tbsp. of a nut butter (almond, hazelnut, cashew)
- ◆ half an avocado (makes the smoothie thick and creamy)
- ◆ 1 tbsp. unrefined coconut oil
- ◆ ginger root
- ◆ turmeric root
- ◆ cinnamon or cardamom
- ◆ raw cacao powder
- ◆ ice
- ◆ protein powder*

---

* Because quality varies greatly, and individual needs for the type and amount of protein vary, check with a healthcare professional with training in nutrition. In general, the best protein powders are made by nutraceutical companies and only sold through licensed healthcare professionals. Check out my personal favorites at www.feedyourmindwellness.com/ under Resources/Brands We Trust.

GUT HEALING BONE BROTH

Ingredients

- bones from a whole pasture-raised chicken carcass (meat removed)
- 8–10 cups of water
- 1–2 tbsp. of fresh lemon juice or raw apple cider vinegar
- 1–2 tsp. salt
- ½ tsp. pepper
- 2 carrots
- 1 onion
- 2 stalks celery
- ½ cup fresh parsley chopped or 2 tbsp. dried parsley
- 1–2 tsp. sage
- 1–2 tsp. rosemary
- 1–2 tsp. thyme
- 2–3 bay leaves

Method

1. Put all ingredients into a large pot and bring to boil or place in a slow cooker.
2. Let simmer on low for several hours (4–24) or in a slow cooker on low for 24–36 hours.
3. Remove the bones and vegetables, strain and skim off surface fat.

Uses for broth:

- Use as stock for soup.
- Drink as a warm beverage.
- Use as the cooking liquid for vegetables.
- Make gravy from the fats.

Adapted from a recipe by Liz Lipski, PhD, CCN

APPENDIX III
7-Day Character Strengths Diary

- Option 1: How will you use your strengths today?

- Option 2: How did you use your strengths today?

CREATIVITY

Day 1	
Day 2	
Day 3	
Day 4	
Day 5	
Day 6	
Day 7	

CURIOSITY

Day 1	
Day 2	
Day 3	
Day 4	
Day 5	
Day 6	
Day 7	

JUDGMENT

Day 1	
Day 2	
Day 3	
Day 4	
Day 5	
Day 6	
Day 7	

LOVE OF LEARNING

Day 1	
Day 2	
Day 3	
Day 4	
Day 5	
Day 6	
Day 7	

PERSPECTIVE

Day 1	
Day 2	
Day 3	
Day 4	
Day 5	
Day 6	
Day 7	

BRAVERY

Day 1	
Day 2	
Day 3	
Day 4	
Day 5	
Day 6	
Day 7	

PERSEVERANCE

Day 1	
Day 2	
Day 3	
Day 4	
Day 5	
Day 6	
Day 7	

HONESTY

Day 1	
Day 2	
Day 3	
Day 4	
Day 5	
Day 6	
Day 7	

ZEST

Day 1	
Day 2	
Day 3	
Day 4	
Day 5	
Day 6	
Day 7	

LOVE

Day 1	
Day 2	
Day 3	
Day 4	
Day 5	
Day 6	
Day 7	

KINDNESS

Day 1	
Day 2	
Day 3	
Day 4	
Day 5	
Day 6	
Day 7	

SOCIAL INTELLIGENCE

Day 1	
Day 2	
Day 3	
Day 4	
Day 5	
Day 6	
Day 7	

TEAMWORK

Day 1	
Day 2	
Day 3	
Day 4	
Day 5	
Day 6	
Day 7	

FAIRNESS

Day 1	
Day 2	
Day 3	
Day 4	
Day 5	
Day 6	
Day 7	

LEADERSHIP

Day 1	
Day 2	
Day 3	
Day 4	
Day 5	
Day 6	
Day 7	

FORGIVENESS

Day 1	
Day 2	
Day 3	
Day 4	
Day 5	
Day 6	
Day 7	

HUMILITY

Day 1	
Day 2	
Day 3	
Day 4	
Day 5	
Day 6	
Day 7	

PRUDENCE

Day 1	
Day 2	
Day 3	
Day 4	
Day 5	
Day 6	
Day 7	

SELF-REGULATION

Day 1	
Day 2	
Day 3	
Day 4	
Day 5	
Day 6	
Day 7	

APPRECIATION OF BEAUTY/EXCELLENCE

Day 1	
Day 2	
Day 3	
Day 4	
Day 5	
Day 6	
Day 7	

GRATITUDE

Day 1	
Day 2	
Day 3	
Day 4	
Day 5	
Day 6	
Day 7	

HOPE

Day 1	
Day 2	
Day 3	
Day 4	
Day 5	
Day 6	
Day 7	

HUMOR

Day 1	
Day 2	
Day 3	
Day 4	
Day 5	
Day 6	
Day 7	

SPIRITUALITY

Day 1	
Day 2	
Day 3	
Day 4	
Day 5	
Day 6	
Day 7	